Thomas Clarkson and Campaign Against Slavery

The life of Thomas Clarkson shows us that one dedicated person can make a real difference to the lives of millions. For sixty years, he was the driving force behind the campaign to end the horrors of slavery. It took Clarkson's vision and persistence to turn the fight against slavery into the leading political issue of the day.

Through his efforts, the abolition campaign was on everyone's mind from 1785 until after the end of the slave trade in the British Empire in 1807 and the full emancipation of British slaves in 1834. In turn, Clarkson was honoured for 'the merit of originating .. the triumph of the great struggle for the deliverance of the enslaved African'.

Thomas Clarkson and the Campaign Against Slavery is published to celebrate the 150th anniversary of the death of one of the world's first human rights activists and 'one of the noblest of Englishmen'.

Zerbanoo Gifford

Dedicated to
Michael Harris and the Quaker Community

First published in Great Britain 1996 by
Anti-Slavery International
The Stableyard
Broomgrove Road
LONDON SW9 9TL
Telephone: +44 (0) 171 924 9555
Fax: +44 (0) 171 738 4110
E.mail: antislavery @gn.apc.org

Pre-press production: Advanced Design of Weasenham
Printed in Great Britain by
The Lanceni Press
Fakenham
Norfolk

Photographic acknowledgements
A Coffle: Mary Evans Picture Library
Death of Captain Ferrer: Library of Congress, Washington
Cutting Sugar Cane: British Library Reproductions
Medal: The Board of Trustees of the National Museums & Galleries on Merseyside
        (Liverpool Museum)

Acknowledgements

One of the reasons for Clarkson's relative obscurity today is that historians have had little material to work on. During his lifetime Clarkson wrote a great many letters and notes as part of his campaigning. Such documents are the primary source material which historians and biographers draw on when they come to research the past. Unfortunately, Clarkson destroyed most of his papers before his death in order, he said, to save the time of the person who would carry out his will. It is interesting to note that historians of the future may well face many similar problems, as the Clarksons of today use the telephone and email to communicate where they would have once written letters.

Clarkson's own modesty might also have played a part in his decision to destroy his papers. His wife related to a friend how: 'My husband is a great destroyer and especially of anything complimentary to himself'. Researchers of the life and works of Thomas Clarkson and his younger brother John owe a great deal to the efforts of Ellen Gibson Wilson. Her books, *John Clarkson and the African Adventure* (1980) and *Thomas Clarkson, a Biography* (1989) are highly recommended for further reading.

Cameos: Thomas Clarkson (left) and his younger brother John

Introduction by
Anti-Slavery International

Several important anniversaries relevant to anti-slavery campaigners are marked in 1996. It is 150 years since the death of Thomas Clarkson who, along with William Wilberforce, persuaded the British people and government to end the slave trade and slavery. Clarkson, described as 'one of the noblest of Englishmen', pioneered many of today's campaigning and lobbying methods in his life-long commitment to the abolition movement. His life will be commemorated with the unveiling of a plaque in Westminster Abbey on 26th September 1996, the exact anniversary of his death.

It is the 100th anniversary of the abolition of slave ownership in the African colonies of France. It is also the 70th anniversary of the first international treaty on the abolition of slavery in all its forms – the United Nations Slavery Convention of 1926 – and the 40th anniversary of the second international treaty on the abolition of slavery – the 1956 United Nations Supplementary Convention on the Abolition of Slavery, the Slave Trade, and Institutions and Practices Similar to Slavery.

Slavery and the slave trade were the first violations of human rights to receive the attention of the international community. Although most people have some knowledge about slavery, they often consider it to be an historic problem, not one of today too. Sadly, this means that the present-day forms of slavery remain both little understood and inadequately researched; also there are insufficient resources for abolition campaigns. However, the current interest in child slavery, forced labour, debt bondage, servile marriage, sexual tourism and trafficking would suggest that people are concerned about contemporary forms of slavery, even if they are not aware of the grand scale on which this system of oppression continues to operate.

The development of the campaign against the slave trade in the Eighteenth Century was closely related to the growth in awareness concerning human rights. It was driven by individuals who had the energy, the courage and the inspiration to devote themselves to the cause in both the public and private domain. This tradition of individual conviction and commitment continues today and is no less controversial or dangerous. These individuals, like Clarkson, need the weight of public opinion behind their cause if they are to effectively highlight and support the daily struggle which the millions of people treated like slaves are undergoing in order to free themselves from oppressive social regimes and cycles of exploitation.

In the 1990's human rights and campaigns for equality figure strongly in debates about global development; we are bombarded daily with statistics of suffering and television images of brutality and oppression. Although we are all moved by these sights and facts, often we do not know how we can channel our convictions into worthwhile action. Anti-Slavery International wishes to educate, inspire and motivate people to see slavery as a current human rights issue to which they can make a valuable contribution. There is a real need to build on public awareness concerning slavery today, developing an appreciation of the wider ideas of human rights, as well as of the ability of individuals to tackle what sometimes appear to be impossible odds in order to achieve social change.

Anti-Slavery International receives a constant stream of enquiries about slavery from children and teachers, mostly in an historical context. Yet it is also aware that in many countries the issue of slavery is poorly dealt with or simply avoided in the school curriculum. Given that slavery has shaped the moral and cultural contours of the modern world and that practices akin to slavery are widespread today and still affect the lives of millions of people, this issue clearly merits more attention and action. Anti-Slavery International aims to provide more information about slavery throughout history and to offer people examples of positive action against this system of subjugation.

By seeking to forget the horrors of slavery in the Eighteenth and Nineteenth centuries, we are in danger of allowing this same system of abuse to flourish today without international protest and resistance. Slavery is not only a crucial aspect of our history, it is a pressing reality of our present. If the beliefs in equality and freedom which are so highly prized by people in Britain, Europe and the West can be directed in the campaign to abolish slavery today, then the Twenty-first Century could be a time when the lives of millions and the course of history will be changed again.

There seems little doubt that slavery has always existed. The subjugation of people for economic ends was common to the ancient civilisations of the Greeks and Romans. Indeed, many of the world's most admired achievements have been built upon slavery. The imposing pyramids of Egypt, the inspiring American Dream of great opportunity, and the now globally expansive capitalist system were created by sacrificing the freedoms and the lives of many. Yet our most ready association with slavery remains the Atlantic slave trade of the Eighteenth and Nineteenth centuries in which millions of African people were taken from their homelands and transported to the Americas and the West Indies, to a life of labour and of bondage. This era of slavery is certainly not the proudest moment in British history, but it is one which yields information and questions which remain worthwhile and relevant today.

One of the major problems in researching the history of slavery is that nearly all accounts of the trade have been written by white people, and are therefore strongly influenced by their perspective. Slaves were often forbidden to write, and even when they did produce their own versions of the slave experience these were discredited and neglected. Even today, records of slavery written by white people (often slave owners) are to be found in libraries under the title 'history' whereas the black slaves' own works are, if available at all, to be found under 'literature'. In very general terms then, the white version of slavery is still taken to be fact and the black version to be fiction. As more slave texts and other sources are being uncovered, there is increasing evidence to suggest that the slaves would have given a very different account of the slave era to most white people, even abolitionists. In particular, the slavery debate has recently focused on the role which the black slaves played in ending their own oppression. The resistance of the slaves may have been underplayed by campaigners both for and against slavery in Britain, as rebellious Africans did not conform to the necessary images of live cargo or oppressed souls. When we consider the remarkable achievements of the abolition movement, and of Thomas Clarkson, we must not overlook the active participation of slaves in overthrowing the system which had sought to deny them home, family and identity.

Another major point of historical debate centres on whether Britain's abolition of slavery was a great sacrifice or a convenient release. It has been suggested that no country would voluntarily end a trade which generated so much profit and that the value of slavery to Britain was decreasing. However, others are convinced that Britain knew that there would be a financial cost to abolition, but believed it to be a price worth paying to end the barbarous exploitation of fellow human beings. In reality it was probably neither entirely an economic nor moral decision, but a move affected by both factors. Moreover, the fact that the costs of slavery were rising and the prices of its commodities falling does not discount the powerful tide of public opinion against the oppressive and systematic abuse of huge African slave populations which was expressed in Britain.

Thomas Clarkson was actively involved in opposing slavery on both moral and economic grounds. He was the first to point out the hidden costs to Britain, such as the fatalities among sailors considered 'expendable' by slave ship owners who were only concerned with keeping their human cargo alive long enough to sell. It was, and is, widely believed that Clarkson's arguments in such debates were decisive.

To his contemporaries, Thomas Clarkson was the driving force behind the campaign to end the horrors of slavery. It took Clarkson's vision and persistence to turn the fight against slavery into the leading political issue of the day. Through the efforts of this man, the abolition campaign was on everyone's mind from 1785 until after the end of the slave trade in the British Empire in 1807 and the full emancipation of British slaves in 1834. His researches unmasked the violence inherent in the whole operation of the slave trade before a horrified public. His great personal effort was instrumental in ensuring that the compassion of the majority of people in Britain outweighed the self-interest of a few.

One of Clarkson's main assets was his single-minded determination. He was resolute that the campaign would succeed and a friend noted that: 'Once he is convinced that something should be done, it is impossible to convince him that it cannot be done'. Another friend, the Romantic poet Samuel Taylor Coleridge, declared that: 'I have called him the moral steam-engine, or the Giant with one idea'. As these tributes suggest, Clarkson was a great believer both in the 'idea' that slavery should end and in the ability of individuals to create lasting change. He realised that he had to awaken people's consciences and change their attitudes, and to do this he adopted and improved a variety of methods which brought otherwise diverse groups together behind a single magnificent cause. Under his guidance, the demand for abolition became an urgent issue which united people from all walks of life. The abolitionists, as they were known, were the first modern 'pressure group', trying to influence government by mobilising public opinion to demand change.

Clarkson's pioneering genius was his awareness that an entirely new set of campaigning tools offered the best way to win the fight. His strategies for fighting slavery meant that everyone could become involved in some way. Although women could not vote or sign petitions at this time, they could wear anti-slavery cameos to show their solidarity with the cause. People could buy the Wedgwood image of a slave in chains and draw attention to the question: 'Am I Not a Man and a Brother?', on everything from their plates to their snuff boxes. The Romantic poets wrote passionately in support of the moral strength of the campaign and, along with others, refused to take slave-produced sugar in their drinks.

As in so many other ways, Clarkson was ahead of his time in his campaigns against 'flags of convenience' (where unscrupulous ship owners avoid the laws of their own country by registering their vessels in another). Although a deacon in the Church of England at a time when religious intolerance and prejudice were enshrined in British law, he worked towards abolition with people of all faiths, particularly the Quakers. He was also one of the first supporters of equality for women, proposing that women should be as well educated as men and be permitted to join the professions – even the clergy.

Clarkson's quest to enlist public support for the abolitionist cause led him to lobby Kings and Emperors, and these men of power declared that it was his publications and personal persuasion which increased their resolve to see an end to slavery. Indeed, Clarkson's internationalism was made clear by his links with many other countries. He volunteered to travel to France at the height of their revolution to increase support for the French abolition movement. He was one of the British philanthropists who helped to found the settlement for freed slaves in 1787, in what is now the African nation of Sierra Leone. He advised King Henry I of Haiti, who faced the difficult and challenging task of rebuilding the social and economic structures of the first independent West Indian state in the aftermath of slavery and civil war. Clarkson lobbied internationally on Haiti's behalf and against slavery at every opportunity. His status and influence can be measured by the fact that when the campaign against slavery started to grow in the United States, it was to Clarkson that the movement's leaders turned for advice and endorsement.

Clarkson always had the advantage of the moral argument that each and every human being should be free. However, he made sure that he could also win any debate on the practical and financial issues involved in ceasing the profitable slave trade. The depth of his knowledge on this subject was recognised as unparalleled, and was the result of many months of personal investigation during which he interviewed over twenty thousand people associated with the slave trade on his long rides around Britain. In order to counter the propaganda of slavers which told how Africans were ignorant savages, Clarkson took with him a chest of fine African-made goods to demonstrate their culture and skills, as well as the potential for fair trade with Africa.

Some of the images which Clarkson produced in order to communicate the horrors of slavery to the public, such as the print of a ship with slaves packed like sardines or, in his own words 'stacked like books on shelves', are still familiar today. Clarkson toured Britain incessantly, researching the slave trade and encouraging the campaign against it, and it was the abolitionist mission which he was eager to promote rather than his own fame or fortune. As a consequence, Clarkson's own name has tended to be forgotten, although his tactics for achieving success have lived on. Today, many other campaigns adopt his techniques. Indeed, when pressure groups use emotive images to encourage people to sign petitions, join local groups and start boycotts, they are following in the abolitionists' footsteps.

Yet all Clarkson's invaluable work came about as a result of chance. Until he entered and won an essay competition at Cambridge University on the rights and wrongs of slavery, he fully expected to dedicate his life to a career in the Church of England.

Thomas Clarkson, first President of Anti-Salvery International

Anti-Slavery International (ASI) is the world's oldest human rights organisation, founded in 1839 with Thomas Clarkson as its first President. It has consultative status at the United Nations.

Through its extensive research programme, collaborating with grass-root groups fighting slavery in their own countries, ASI has drawn the world's attention to the fact that slavery is still occurring all over the world.

ASI is currently working worldwide on bonded labour of adults and children, child prostitution, trafficking in women and children, forced labour and more. Slavery even exists in Britain, with unscrupulous employers taking advantage of overseas domestic servants.

The author's royalties will go towards ASI's work to help end child bonded labour.

The Old Grammar School in Hill Street, Wisbech (c. 1895), birthplace of Thomas and John. Their father, John Clarkson, was Headmaster until his premature death in 1766 (aged 55)

No 8 York Row, Wisbech: Thomas and John lived here with their sister and widowed mother for most of their childhood years

Thomas Clarkson

Thomas Clarkson was born in Wisbech, Cambridgeshire, on 28th March 1760, the third child of John and Anne Clarkson. His father was a curate at a local parish and headmaster of Wisbech's grammar school. Three days after Thomas' sixth birthday, John Clarkson died suddenly, having caught a fever from a sick parishioner he had visited. The young Thomas studied at his late father's school until he was fifteen, when he went to St Paul's School in London. At that time, St Paul's was housed next to the great cathedral and was more renowned for its harsh discipline than the academic success of its pupils. Despite this, Thomas Clarkson's academic ability was clear and he won two scholarships to St John's, the Cambridge college where his father had studied. It was expected that Thomas would follow his father in becoming a priest, and one of his schoolmasters even predicted that he would rise to become a bishop in the Church of England. In 1783, as a first step on this road, Clarkson was ordained deacon in Winchester, having received an honours degree from Cambridge.

However, Clarkson's scholarly interests remained strong and, as a graduate studying for his masters degree at Cambridge, Clarkson was eligible to enter the University's Latin essay competitions. In 1784, he was awarded first prize in one competition and entered for a second, determined to become the first person to win two essay prizes. The essay question was set by the Vice-Chancellor, Dr Peckard, who was an opponent of the slave trade. The question which he chose, *'Anne liceat invitos in servitutem dare?'* ('Is it right to enslave men against their will?'), was a brave one given the fact that Cambridge colleges received substantial donations from slave-owners and from their own investments

Clarkson had only two months to research his essay and, at his own admittance, he knew almost nothing of the subject before he began. He also acknowledged how lucky he was to find Anthony Benezet's *Some Historical Account of Guinea ... with an Inquiry into the Rise and Progress of the Slave Trade*. This book written by an American Quaker, greatly impressed Clarkson, who wrote: 'In this precious book I found almost all I wanted'. Indeed, it was Benezet's book which had previously influenced Granville Sharp, probably the first man to bring the issue of slavery to the attention of the British public. Sharp was willing to challenge the legal system, and brought a succession of cases involving gross injustices against black slaves in an attempt to force the courts to declare slavery illegal in Britain. His efforts to effect the abolition of slavery also need to be acknowledged.

Granville Sharp's Legal Battles

Granville Sharp (1735 - 1813) is commonly regarded to be the father of the abolitionist cause. Like Clarkson, Sharp came from a religious family, his father was an archdeacon and his grandfather an archbishop. Indeed, he was regarded as somewhat eccentric for choosing to be a junior civil servant rather than to join the more highly regarded professions of his brothers.

In 1765, Sharp visited his brother William, a surgeon, and was struck by the sight of a young black man in the queue for treatment. He was clearly extremely ill, having been beaten so badly that he could barely stand or see. Sharp was moved into action and having taken this young man into the surgery in front of the other patients, he stayed with him while his brother treated him. They discovered that his name was Jonathan Strong and that he had been brought to London as a slave from Barbados by his owner, David Lisle, a lawyer. Lisle had beaten Strong with a pistol until it had broken in pieces and had then thrown him onto the streets, as he would have done a useless possession. As a result of this vicious attack Strong spent four months in St Bartholomew's Hospital where he recovered sufficient health to leave, and Sharp helped to find him a job.

All seemed to have ended happily for Strong, but two years later, in 1767, his former owner, Lisle, spotted him by chance in the street. He was amazed to see Strong still alive, and promptly hired two slave hunters to kidnap him. Lisle still believed he owned Strong and sold him for £30 to James Kerr, a plantation owner who planned to send him to the West Indies. But before he set sail, Strong managed to send a note to Sharp detailing what had happened. Sharp went straight to the courts and accused Kerr of kidnap. The case was heard by the Lord Mayor of London who declared that since Strong 'had not stolen anything and was not guilty of any offence' he was 'thus at liberty to go away'. Yet the captain of the ship which was waiting to transport Strong to the West Indies could not believe this verdict in favour of a slave and grabbed Strong's arm to take him away. Sharp ordered him to stop, or be charged with assault. As Sharp later wrote in his diary: 'The Captain thereupon withdrew his hand, and all parties retired from the presence of the Lord Mayor. And Jonathan Strong departed also, in the sight of all, in full liberty, nobody daring afterwards to touch him'.

However, even this episode did not mark the end of this ordeal. Lisle challenged Sharp to a duel (which he refused), and Kerr sued him for 'robbing the original master of his slave' and for the £30 Strong had cost him. Although Sharp's solicitors told him that he would lose the case and advised him to pay the money, he refused to be intimidated and, after studying the relevant laws himself, he finally formed a response which led Kerr to drop the case.

Even though he was now indisputably a free man, Jonathan Strong fell ill again five years later. He died aged just 25, due to the injuries which he had sustained during the beating by Lisle. Although Strong was just one of millions of slaves whose lives were cut short by their brutal treatment, he is remembered today because of the chance meeting with Granville Sharp and the legal campaign that marked the beginning of the end of slavery in the British Empire.

For Sharp, the defence of all slaves urgently needed to be mounted and he remained determined to compel the courts to declare slavery in Britain illegal. Since Kerr had withdrawn his case, Sharp looked for another example of injustice to make a test case (a legal case which determines what the law actually is when it is unclear). He did not have long to wait. In 1771, Thomas Lewis, was kidnapped by his former owner and chained to the mast of a ship bound for Jamaica. Word of this outrage against a fellow man reached Sharp who swiftly obtained a legal writ to stop the ship sailing. Fortunately, unfavourable winds had prevented the voyage and the officer of the courts managed to serve the writ. This officer later described seeing Lewis gagged, to stop him screaming out in protest at his treatment, with tears streaming down his face at the knowledge of his reprieve.

Lewis' case was heard before Lord Mansfield who, as the Lord Chief Justice, was Britain's top judge. Mansfield was himself a slave owner, and one of his slaves in London, Elisabeth Dido Lindsay, was the daughter of his nephew. As such, it is unsurprising that he was determined to avoid the underlying issue of whether slavery was lawful in Britain. Mansfield commented: 'Perhaps it is much better that it should never be discussed or settled, ... I don't know what the consequences may be, if the masters were to lose their property by accidentally bringing their slaves to England'. Once again, slaves were being taken to be mere possessions with no individual rights or freedoms.

However, the jury in the case decided that Lewis was a free man who should not have been kidnapped. This verdict was received with delight by many in the public gallery who cried out: 'No property! No property!' Nevertheless, despite the jury's decision to declare Lewis a free man, Mansfield managed to avoid making the case apply to all slaves in Britain.

Sharp remained steadfast in his legal campaign for abolition and he soon met Mansfield in court again. This time, the case was that of James Somerset, who had been brought to Britain from Virginia, USA as a slave, but had escaped. Again, his former owner, Charles Steward, had recaptured him and was trying to send him to the West Indies, when Sharp obtained a writ to prevent this.

The case began in December 1771. Lawyers hired by Sharp argued that a slave could only be treated as a slave where this practice was legal. In the Americas, many laws allowed slavery, but no British law did so. Moreover, since British law did not recognise slavery, once Somerset arrived in Britain, he could no longer be deemed a slave. In order to illustrate his point, one lawyer asked: 'Have the laws of Virginia any more influence, power or authority in this country than the laws of Japan?' This was difficult for Mansfield to deny, so he adjourned the case for several months and tried to persuade Somerset's former owner to accept his loss and free Somerset in the hope that he could avoid a ruling applicable to all slaves in Britain. Steward refused and the case resumed. Finally, in June 1772, Mansfield gave his verdict: 'A foreigner cannot be imprisoned here on the authority of any law existing in his own country ... No master was ever allowed here to take a slave by force to be sold abroad because he deserted from his service, or for any other reason'.

Somerset and his champion Sharp had won the case and it was widely reported that this successful 'test case' had put an end to slavery in Britain. An estimated ten thousand slaves held in Britain were freed as a result of the publicity, although many others continued to be sold or shipped to plantations in the West Indies. In fact this conclusion was too hasty and Mansfield had managed once more to avoid ruling that slavery, as such, was illegal in Britain. For many years afterwards newspapers in Britain continued to carry advertisements for the sale of slaves and many slaves received harsh and violent treatment at the hands of their owners.

In 1793, Lord Mansfield died. Despite his earlier refusal to rule that all slaves in Britain be released, he had ensured that his will contained explicit instructions to free Elisabeth Dido Lindsay, the slave fathered by his nephew. Mansfield was buried in Westminster Abbey, a respected member of British Society.

Sharp was also known for his legal case concerning the slave ship Zong in 1787. The owners of this vessel tried to claim compensation for their financial loss when 131 sick slaves were thrown overboard by the ship's crew. After a voyage which had taken months rather than weeks, the Captain of the Zong murdered the slaves in the belief that the insurers would compensate for loss rather than for damage to the 'cargo'. However, the insurers refused to pay on the grounds that they were not liable for deaths resulting from illness. Had the slaves been murdered for rebelling, they would have paid up without complaint. Slaves, it was said plainly in court, were merely property, not people, and it was 'madness' to think otherwise.

As a result of Sharp's interest in this incident an Act of Parliament was passed in 1788 to introduce a measure of regulation over conditions on board slave ships. This was only a minor achievement for the man who wished slavery to be outlawed. Granville Sharp may not have won the legal victory which he worked so tirelessly towards, but he did succeed in laying down the moral and political foundations of the abolitionist cause. It was upon these solid foundations that Thomas Clarkson built his own campaign.

Studying the Realities of Slavery

Clarkson had expected his essay to be an academic exercise, 'an innocent contest for literary honour', but he found himself increasingly drawn into the subject as he read more about it. During the two months he spent researching and writing his essay, Clarkson found it difficult to sleep, as his mind dealt with the nightmarish horrors of the slave trade. He was relieved when he finally handed in his competition piece, and left Cambridge for London. Through his scholarly activity, Clarkson was to discover that Britain was deeply involved in the slave trade and that the details of this involvement were both horrific and morally disturbing.

Britain sent ships to the coast of Africa to obtain slaves against their will, then transported them across the Atlantic to work in its colonies in America and the West Indies, finally importing the cash crops of sugar, tobacco and cotton these colonies were forced to grow back to Britain. This cycle was known as the 'triangular trade', and while each leg of the voyage could be extremely profitable for the British, it proved fatal for the many Africans who did not survive the Middle Passage to the 'New World'.

Mortality on the slave ships was high, at least one in twenty died; most due to a loss of fluids through diarrhoea caused by 'the flux' (dysentery). We now know that good hygiene is vital to control the spread of dysentery but this was impossible in the extremely cramped conditions on the slave ships. One ship's surgeon described: 'The deck, that is the floor of their rooms, was so covered with blood and mucus which had proceeded from them in consequence of the flux that it resembled a slaughter-house ... It is not in the power of human imagination, to picture itself a situation more dreadful or disgusting'.

The survivors of this nightmare voyage were often left permanently weakened and even after landing in the West Indies, slaves continued to die in huge numbers, despite the best efforts of doctors. As these slaves were now precious and profitable commodities if alive and working, on some islands each doctor had fewer people to treat than a GP working in Britain today. Nevertheless, the fact that between a quarter and a third of African slaves died within three years of arriving on the plantations is a clear indication of the truly appalling conditions which slaves were forced to endure. The biggest killers were 'dropsy' (now known as beriberi) which is a disease is caused by an inadequate diet, fevers, the 'flux' and yaws. The last two thrived in the insanitary conditions, whilst dropsy was at its worst when slaves were forced to go hungry between the processing of the sugar harvest in June and the planting of the new crop in August and September. This situation was made worse when greedy plantation owners converted even the small plots of land set aside for slaves to cultivate their own food into sugar producing fields.

The arduous work on the plantations began at dawn and lasted for up to fourteen hours, six days a week. In the evenings and on their one day off, Sunday, slaves were expected to be able to grow enough food to feed themselves throughout the week. As if this daily torment did not enact sufficient hardship and deprivation, slaves were frequently sold to other masters regardless of their family or marital attachments, and children were sold away from mothers.

As plantation owners were prepared to pay a higher price for male slaves, 'on account of the superior strength and labour of the men', most ships carried twice as many men as women. Even so, the hard physical work in the fields was mostly done by women, who were not trained for most of the skilled and semi-skilled positions on the plantations. Indeed, becoming a domestic (household) slave was the only alternative to field work for women.

Pregnant slaves were kept working until around six weeks before they were due, and typically had to resume work three weeks after they gave birth. It is not surprising that a quarter of children born to slave women died within a week, and it is estimated that another quarter died within their first year. Even in an age when child mortality was very high by modern standards, these were shocking statistics. As soon as children could walk, they were put to work alongside their mother. One manual for slave-owners advised that: 'Each child should have a little basket, and be made somewhat useful by gathering up fallen trash and leaves, and pulling up weeds'.

With such a high mortality rate and low birth rate, the West Indies continued to demand more and more new slaves. Although other islands made jokes about Barbados having a 'plague' of women, both black and white, it was this island which demonstrated an alternative to the trade in new lives. Although conditions for slaves on Barbados remained poor, they were the best in the region with opportunities for marriage; as a result the slaves were more fertile and the island's imports of new African slaves declined. This became particularly important after 1807 when the slave trade was abolished but the slaves already working in the colonies had not been set free.

The white population throughout the West Indies was heavily outnumbered by their slaves, in order to maintain order and exert their authority the masters ruled by fear and denied all rights to the slaves. These African slaves faced a relentless variety of punishments, from whippings in the field for 'laziness' to mutilation, torture and death for anything from running away or theft, to fighting back or simply being accused of plotting against their owner. An owner who accidentally killed a slave 'shall not be liable to any penalty or forfeiture whatsoever', one law stated. Since slaves could not give evidence against their owners or any other white person, this left them with no protection against murder except their economic value as workers. One island's laws made this belief perfectly clear: 'The Rights of a Master be every Thing, and those of the Slave nothing'. When slaves were executed, their bodies would usually be left to rot in sight of their companions so as to draw attention to the high price of even minor insubordination. The sum of this systematic subjugation and degradation of African slaves was the denial of their very right to humanity.

While the terrible consequences of slavery upon the lives of the Africans wrenched from their homelands and forced into bondage should not be forgotten, it is also important to remember the remarkable acts of resistance and of creative expression which occurred even given these conditions. The armed slave rebellions were evidently the most extreme and violent episodes of resistance. These continued throughout the period of enslavement and occurred on almost every colony. One of the most well-organised, fierce and successful rebellions was the Maroon war in Jamaica which ended in 1740. The free community of Maroons (runaway slaves) fought the English under the leadership of Nanny, an Ashanti priestess, to preserve their 600 acres of land and, most importantly, win their freedom. However, resistance to a master's orders was also demonstrated in more subtle ways. It is now believed that the frequent complaints about the laziness of the slaves are accounts of a deliberate 'go slow' policy on the part of enslaved labourers who did not dare to refuse to work and yet demonstrated their resistance by working as little and as slowly as possible, or by feigning illness.

Keeping alive memories and traditions from Africa was also a mode of resistance. In their work-songs, spirituals, folk-tales and proverbs, slaves were able to preserve elements of the oral cultures which they brought with them from their African homelands. However, in these creative expressions, Africans were also creating new cultural forms which developed from the mixing of different African languages, belief systems, memories and practices, and which emerged from their new circumstances as slaves in the West Indies or America. These new folk cultures which encompassed song, stories, worship and dance nurtured the spirits and minds of Africans whose bodies were being broken by slavery. They also teach us that slaves did find a voice and ways to express their hopes and affections, as well as their anguish and pain. Indeed, these acts of cultural expression were incredibly important in preserving and creating a sense of identity and tradition in the face of an inhumane system of exploitation which sought to deny the black slaves their personhood and any sense of community.

Given the fact that slaves were treated as less than human, the literary works of African slaves and ex-slaves are important documents which testify to great creative and spiritual resources and the successful struggle to be heard against enormous odds. However, finding the education, the courage and the will to write was not all that was involved for an African to be accepted as a writer. The American slave, Phillis Wheatley who published a book of poetry in 1773, could only have her work published once she had obtained an 'Attestation', which was a written notice from a group of Boston's most highly esteemed citizens supporting and verifying the work as her own. Even after this was acquired, many people could not believe that an African could write poetry. In fact, the literary endeavours of slaves and freed slaves were an important tool in the abolitionist cause. The very fact that these people could read and write and produce literary works significantly weakened the pro-slavery argument that Africans were naturally intellectually inferior to Europeans and therefore suited to enslavement.

It is probably the slave narratives, which tell of their authors' journeys from slavery to freedom and detail the cruelty and injustice of their treatment as slaves, which were most closely connected to the abolitionist cause. We already know of over one hundred slave narratives; the better known of these are *The Interesting Narrative of the Life of Olaudah Equiano* (1789) and the *Narrative of the Life of Frederick Douglass, an American Slave* (1845). Although the majority of slave narratives were written by men, two narratives by women are seen to be especially important. Harriet Jacobs' *Incidents in the Life of a Slave Girl* (1861) is significant because it highlights the sexual vulnerability particular to female slaves. Although Jacobs is careful not to include any details which might offend a white readership, her narrative offers a strong sense of the double degradation, as both material and sexual possessions, which female slaves had to endure at the hands of their masters.

The History of Mary Prince, A West Indian Slave, Related by Herself which was published in London and Edinburgh in 1831 was sponsored by the Anti-Slavery Society. The organisation's magazine, *The Anti-Slavery Reporter*, often chronicled the sufferings of slaves in order to further public support for the abolitionist campaign. While these representations of black oppression served an important political function, it was vital that black people represented themselves and told their own stories. This is exactly what Mary Prince was able to do in her slave narrative which told of her different treatment under five masters and of her conscious acts of rebellion against the cruelty and advances of these men. Born in Bermuda but sold to the Turks islands and then Antigua, Mary Prince finally managed to free herself from her last vindictive owners, the Woods, in London in 1827. Having escaped slavery herself, Mary Prince was anxious to work to free other slaves, as she wrote: 'In telling my own sorrows, I cannot pass by those of my fellow-slaves - for when I think of my own griefs, I remember theirs'. Prince became involved with the anti-slavery campaign and with their support and guidance wrote her moving life story which ends with a strident plea to the British people: 'I hope they will never leave off to pray God, and call loud to the great King of England, till all the poor blacks be given free, and slavery done up for evermore.'

The Interesting Life of Olaudah Equiano

Equiano Olaudah was born in Essaka, Eboe [now the Eastern part of Nigeria], the son of a elder and priest. At the age of ten he was captured by African slave handlers along with his sister and sold to slave traders in the Niger Delta. Although he did not know it then, Equiano was never to see his native homeland or his family again.

During his childhood and adolescence, Equiano was sold several times and journeyed to the West Indies, England, as well as to Canada and the Mediterranean when he was bought by Pascal, a naval captain. As was common practice, Equiano was renamed by his slave masters, first Michael, then Jacob, and then, by Lieutenant Pascal, the classical Gustavus Vassa after the Swedish King. Even though he had previously promised his loyal servant his freedom, it was Pascal who sold Equiano on to Robert King, a Quaker from Philadelphia. King treated Equiano

A Slave Remembers

Of those who wrote first-hand accounts of the slave-trade merchants in the slaving-ports - hard-drinking factors on the Guinea coast, sea-captains and tough slave-owners - few said anything about the slaves themselves. There were, however, a few slaves who knew, or learned how to write and who could fill this gap. The most famous of these was Olaudah Equiano, renamed Gustavus Vassa by his master, who became active in the British anti-slavery campaign. Born in what is now Nigeria, son of the headman of a village, Vassa was kidnapped as a child, transported to Barbados, and later bought by an Englishman from whom he regained his freedom. In 1789 his memoirs were published in London.

Workhouse treadmill J M Phillippo, *Jamaica*, 1843

Boiling sugar, Trinidad R Bridgens 1836

with some respect and he was granted certain privileges unusual for slaves. He worked for King as a seaman, servant and clerk and managed to accumulate some capital from his small scale trading in ports. During his service, Equiano was able to save the £40 to buy his freedom and requested his manumission from King. Although a Quaker and a man of his word, King was reluctant to let the intelligent and loyal Equiano go and had to be persuaded by Thomas Farmer, Equiano's captain and a mutual friend.

In 1766 at the age of twenty-one, Equiano returned to a life at sea as a free man. For many years he sailed around the Mediterranean and voyaged to the Mosquito Coast of Central America, and to the Arctic. In London, Equiano was active in the scheme to enable the city's poor black population to live in the free African territory of Sierra Leone in 1786. He was given the role as Commissary for Stores and was an important figure in communications between the white and black communities. However, Equiano was seen to be too persistent in his pursuit of justice and too morally superior in his arguments; eventually he made himself so unpopular that he was dismissed from the project and so failed to return to Africa.

One positive consequence to emerge from this was that in 1789 Equiano published his life story in the form of a slave narrative entitled *The Interesting Narrative of the Life of Olaudah Equiano or Gustavus Vassa, the African, Written by Himself*, Even though it was published in the same year that the Bastille fell and the French Revolution shook Europe, Equiano's narrative does not employ the revolutionary spirit of its time. Although an active campaigner and spokesperson, Equiano chose not to publish a political pamphlet declaiming the evils of slavery, but rather to write a story which stressed his own humanity and which played upon the feelings of the reader and the appeal to common humanity in the fight against slavery.

In the first chapter of his book Equiano describes his settled and rooted early life in Essaka. He relates the values and customs of his own community: the workings of a democratic and just legal system, the clear social codes concerning marriage, the hard work which produces good agriculture, and the songs and dances which formed part of the communal activity of the village. This portrayal of the rigorous social and moral practices which governed his life in Africa carefully counters the images presented by pro-slavery campaigners, like those of Bernard Romans in 1775: 'Treachery, theft, stubbornness and idleness ... are such consequences of their manner of life at home [in Africa] as to put it out of all doubt that these qualities are neutral to them and not originated by their state of slavery.'

Later on in his book, Equiano appeals to the reader through the universal and fundamental bonds of family relationships, describing how: 'My sister and I were then separated as we lay clasped in each other's arms'. However, Equiano does not only want to convince the reader of the African's essential humanity, but also of his equality. He undertakes the task of bridging the gap between master and slave, white and black, superior and inferior by describing his experiences of slavery and the Middle Passage (the journey from Africa to the New World) from the slave's perspective rather than the slave owner's. Equiano also draws upon his own good fortune at having masters and friends willing to educate him and mostly treat him honourably in order to dramatise the poverty and confinement of slaves lives in general.

The religious context in which the slave narratives were written is important to acknowledge. Equiano was a devout Christian and this faith provided the basis of his appeal to end slavery: 'O, ye nominal Christians! might not an African ask you, Learned you this [slavery] from your God who says unto you, Do unto all men as you would men should do unto you?'. When Equiano describes his first experience of reading the Bible, he exclaims how he was: 'wonderfully surprised to see the laws and rules of my country written almost exactly here'. This suggestion that Ibo society was unwittingly Christian is very important to the abolitionist thread of the narrative, as the practice of buying, selling and owning other Christians was a major point of contention. If Equiano could persuade his reader that Africans were Christian at heart then his argument for the equality of all would be significantly advanced.

The triumph of Equiano's narrative was that it opened the white reader's eyes to prejudice and injustice, but it did so humbly. It made the reader feel the rough hold of slavery, but it did so gently. It allowed the reader to accept the humanity and equality of an African, but it did so with subtlety. His narrative was well-received, although like Phillis Wheatley before him and Mary Prince after, Equiano was thought by some to have had help from a white man in writing his work. In contrast, the Monthly Review declared that: 'The narrative wears an honest face and we have conceived a good opinion of the man'.

It is almost certainly true that Equiano's life and work achieved a popular status because his actions and words were acceptable to British codes of behaviour during this period. Nevertheless, the fact that his story sold so widely, with seventeen editions in thirty years and translations into German, Dutch and Russian, meant that the life of an African had been embraced widely by a white readership.

As a leader and spokesperson for the black community of London, often known as the Sons of Africa, Equiano took part in public debates on slavery and both corresponded and met with key figures in the abolitionist movement. He was on friendly terms with Dr Peckard of Cambridge University and it was perhaps Peckard's acquaintance with Equiano that inspired his choice of slavery as the question for the Cambridge essay competition which Clarkson went on to win. Indeed, it was Equiano who first prompted Granville Sharp to take up the case of the slave ship Zong in court. His letter to Lord Hawkesbury was put forward as evidence in the Parliamentary Enquiry into the Slave Trade (1789) for its persuasive argument in favour of fair trade with Africa. Equiano wrote, in his words, that: 'A commercial intercourse with Africa opens an inexhaustible source of wealth to the manufacturing interest of Great Britain; and to all which the Slave Trade is a physical obstruction... The Abolition of the diabolical Slavery will give most rapid and permanent Extension to Manufactures, which is totally and diametrically opposite to what some interested people assert.'

From the publication of his book to his death in 1797 at the age of 52, Equiano toured the country reading from his narrative and promoting the abolitionist campaign. His supreme dedication to the cause of his fellow Africans can be witnessed by the fact that after his marriage to Susan Cullen, a white woman, in 1792, he spent only ten days with his wife before resuming his campaign work. Although a remarkable man, Equiano was not unique. In his life's work and in his published narrative, he has left us important evidence of the active contribution which African people made to the abolition of slavery.

The Start of the Campaign

In June 1785, it was announced that Clarkson had won the competition. He returned to Cambridge to accept the prize and read his essay to an audience in the university's Senate House. As he rode back to London with the prize money, the subject of slavery would not leave his mind and Clarkson never forgot the moment at which his life changed for ever. Sitting on a hill above Wade's Mill in Hertfordshire, he was struck by a simple but irrefutable conviction: 'If the contents of the Essay were true, it was time some person should see these calamities to the end.' As a result of this moment of vision, Clarkson was to spend the rest of his life dedicated to the campaign against slavery. It is curious to imagine how history may have unfolded rather differently had Dr Peckard chosen a different question for the competition.

Clarkson's first step was to translate his prize-winning essay into English, so that many more people could read and understand it. He took the opportunity to develop the piece and then he started to look for a publisher. During his search he met a Quaker from his home town, Wisbech, who introduced him to the bookseller who had printed most of the anti-slavery works then available. The extended English version of Clarkson's essay was duly published in 1786 as the 256 page book, *An Essay on the Slavery and Commerce of the Human Species, Particularly the African*.

Over the next few months, Clarkson was introduced to the leading figures already engaged in the fight against slavery, including the small committee of Quakers formed in 1787. Clarkson's determination impressed them all, not least a young solicitor, Richard Phillips, who knew both the workings of government and many of the politicians and officials the abolitionists would need to persuade. The two men decided to work together. Their first step was to research the workings of the slave trade.

It was clear that many, many people in Britain had a connection with the slave trade and therefore an interest in its continuation. It could be argued that almost every family had a link with slavery, they may have made the goods that were exchanged for slaves in Africa, or owned plantations in the Americas, or invested in the voyages of the slave ships, or simply used ate, drank and smoked the output of the plantations.

Britain's population demanded the products of slave labour in vast quantities. They were addicted to smoking the tobacco grown in Virginia and Maryland; the colonies' exports had grown from around 22,000 kilos in 1620, to over 450,000 kilos in 1640, reaching ten million kilos in 1775. In this same year, the British West Indies produced 100,000 tonnes of sugar to satisfy the nation's sweet tooth. Sugar was used as an ingredient in cakes and puddings, and a sweetener in the increasingly popular beverages of coffee and chocolate (both also grown using slave labour), as well as in the new national drink, tea. Britain developed new factories, in part to meet the demand from the West Indies and forty per cent of British exports crossed the Atlantic. Britain's exchequer benefited too, collecting duty on the imports of tea and sugar. When the duty on tea was reduced in 1784, tea drinking became even more popular and the demand for sugar to sweeten the bitter taste increased yet again.

Although those in the upper reaches of British Society sneered at what they saw as the coarse manners of the plantation owners, they could not deny that these men made vast fortunes from the trade. Plantation owners used their wealth to buy large estates in Britain, building many of the great country houses, as well as to buy political influence in favour of slavery.

Aware of the climate of acceptance concerning the slave trade and its benefits to Britain, Clarkson set out to interview as many people as possible with experience of the slave trade. With Phillips' help, he obtained access to the records of the customs houses and statistics detailing the numbers of seamen involved. By studying these documents Clarkson discovered that over a fifth of the sailors on board slave ships died on their voyages and another third never returned to Britain for other reasons. The life of a sailor then was acknowledged to be dangerous, but it was a glaring fact that 'every two vessels to Africa would kill more seamen than 83 going to Newfoundland'. Brutalised by the trade themselves, Captains often terrorised their sailors. All too often they dumped sailors in the West Indies on the grounds that fewer hands were needed for the return leg. Sailors also died from dysentery or injuries sustained during slave rebellions. The high mortality rate also reflected the attitude of some ship owners that the life of a slave who could be sold for profit was worth more than that of a sailor, who could easily be replaced at the next port.

One of the witnesses Clarkson met was the Rev John Newton, now best remembered as the author of the hymn 'Amazing Grace'. Newton himself had gone to sea aged ten and was later press-ganged into the Royal Navy. As the Navy did not appreciate his habit of jumping ship to see his childhood sweetheart, after he had been flogged several times, he was exchanged for another sailor on board a slave ship. Newton spent several years working on the coast of Africa, and learnt much about the trade. On his return voyage to Liverpool, he survived a major storm which led to his zealous belief in Christianity.

When Newton was offered the captaincy of a slave ship, he saw no contradiction between his religious beliefs and his active participation in the slave trade, as the Bible does not condemn owning slaves. He set off on a fourteen month voyage to Africa to collect slaves and deliver them to Antigua, before coming back to Britain laden with the island's sugar. By 1754 Newton had retired from the sea and become, like Clarkson, a minister in the Church of England. In his role as a ship's captain, Newton had had no qualms about torturing those slaves he suspected of planning a rebellion and then thanking God for delivering the crew safely from a variety of perils. Now, he joined in the fight against slavery and became William Wilberforce's spiritual adviser.

Wilberforce was a Member of Parliament for Yorkshire, one of the few areas of Britain with no great interest in the slave trade. Its major port, Hull, was the largest in the country not to take part in the trade with Africa and the West Indies. Aged 27, Wilberforce had already been in Parliament for six years and was looking for a cause to champion. He asked his friend, the Prime Minister William Pitt, for advice on whether slavery would be the grand issue or whether an attack on vice in Britain would be better. Pitt suggested that Wilberforce should take up the fight against the slave trade before someone else became its leader inside Parliament. As well as his political connections, Wilberforce's other great asset was his ability to move people with his speeches. The writer James Boswell reflected after attending one of Wilberforce's meetings: 'I saw a little fellow on a table speaking – a perfect shrimp' (his nickname of the 'shrimp' referred both to his small physical size and the fishing interests of Hull), but that as his speech unfolded 'the little fellow grew and grew. And presently the shrimp swelled into a whale'.

Clarkson left a copy of his Essay at Wilberforce's London home, and reading this seems to have been one of the decisive influences in leading Wilberforce to agree that slavery would be the issue for him to champion. 'God Almighty,' Wilberforce declared, 'has set before me two great objects – the abolition of the slave trade and the reformation of manners'. His earlier political choice to champion abolition was now a personal conviction. When Clarkson heard of Wilberforce's decision he himself declared that it was the 'happiest day I had then spent in my life'.

As later events revealed, slavery was one issue that could unite people of otherwise diverse views. While Clarkson was a great supporter of radical change on a number of issues, Wilberforce was more conservative. Indeed, he was the first MP to suggest that the new organisations of working men, the trade unions, should be banned. He also opposed changes to the way the House of Commons was elected. It has been suggested that Wilberforce needed support in mastering the facts and arguments involved in the abolition campaign, and in this respect the scholarly Clarkson was the ideal aid to the charismatic Wilberforce. Clarkson was able to provide huge amounts of information and was also quick to grasp the crucial arguments in the campaign against the slave trade. Despite their different political opinions, the two men would soon prove to be an effective team.

In May 1787, with the prospect of Wilberforce's inspirational voice in Parliament, Clarkson called a meeting of a new group. He acknowledged that the admirable quiet work of the Quaker committee which had been a great help in his researches but suggested that what was needed now was a national organisation to build public support for the abolitionist cause. It would be run by an executive committee based in London and not linked to any one section of society. Clarkson had soon received the agreement of everyone concerned as to the way forward. As well as Clarkson and Phillips, Granville Sharp, the 'father of the cause in England' was invited to join, along with the members of the old Quaker committee.

Tolerance of religions other than the Anglican Church of England was not then a feature of British culture. Prejudice against Roman Catholics in particular was fixed in law. Catholics were banned from professions such as medicine, law and the military, and were also stopped from being MPs or councillors. One law even forbade Catholics from travelling more than five miles from their home without permission. Such religious prejudice was a major problems the old Quaker committee had faced. Their adherence to the Quaker principle of equality between men and absence of social titles often offended non-Quakers in an age when titles were deemed important. Similarly, their refusal to use names of the days and months in their writings (because they were named after Roman and Norse gods or rituals) was also highlighted in order to divert attention from the anti-slavery argument. By appointing an Anglican, Granville Sharp, as chairman, the new committee could avoid all such problems and focus on the urgent matter at hand.

The question of the name for the new organisation was an important one. Were they to campaign against the trade in slaves or against slavery itself? The former would be hard enough to achieve, without taking on the whole institution of slavery. Sharp argued for the latter and 'with a loud voice ... and both hands uplifted to Heaven,' he made the point that slavery itself was the basic evil, and that they would be 'guilty before God' if they did not agree. However the majority felt otherwise and so they became the Committee for Effecting the Abolition of the Slave Trade. It would be the first of what we now call 'pressure groups', organising popular opinion in an attempt to influence government.

Christianity and the Slave Trade

Christianity played an important role in both the rise and fall of Britain's slave trade. Early slave traders used the fact that the Africans were 'pagans' as one of the strongest justifications for enslaving them and made no attempt to convert them to Christianity. During the Eighteenth Century, many people in Britain converted to the new Christian churches such as the Methodists, the Baptists and the Moravians. As these new churches found volunteers and raised funds for missionary work, an interest in converting the slaves in the West Indies developed.

At first slave owners were reluctant to allow their slaves to be baptised and become Christians. One asked the pertinent question: 'Is it Possible that any of my slaves could go to Heaven, and I must meet them there?' Allowing slaves to know the Christian gospel of brotherhood between followers was also seen as dangerous; how could a slave be allowed to think that he was in any way equal to his master? Yet, by badgering the missionaries and preachers, the owners made it clear to their slaves that these newcomers were different from themselves. The slaves followed the simple logic that anyone their owners hated was probably their friend. Nevertheless, some missionaries were given strict instructions not to do anything to upset relations between the slaves and their owners. The Rev John Smith was told by the London Missionary Society that: 'Not a word must escape you in public or private which might render the slaves displeased with their masters or dissatisfied with their station. You are sent not to relieve them from their servile condition, but to afford them the consolations of religion'.

Despite such warnings, the feared consequences of Christian intervention came to pass and tens of thousands of slaves took up the message of equality between believers, both in life and after death. Many were taught to read in order to read the Bible, but it also meant that they could see for themselves the reports of the anti-slavery campaign in newspapers published in the West Indies. In many cases, this new knowledge led to an increase in the number of slave revolts, although some slaves staged peaceful demonstrations. When one new chapel was opened in Jamaica, slaves sat in all the pews and refused to stand up for their white owners, who were thus forced to stand in the aisles during the service.

Other revolts were far more violent. Rev Smith had been sent to Demerara [now Georgetown, capital of Guyana], where a major rebellion broke out in 1823 after a communion service. Three white people were killed and, in retaliation, hundreds of black slaves were executed. In seeking to establish the cause of this rebellion, the slave owners pointed to the work of the missionaries. One slave during the trial proclaimed: 'I solemnly avow that .. had there been no Methodists .. there would have been no revolt'. A British soldier strengthened this argument by reporting that all of the rebel slaves wanted freedom, and that 'all of them dwelt considerably on going to Church on Sunday'. Rev Smith was found guilty of complicity and sentenced to death several months after the rebellion, but he died before he could be hanged. Following the deaths of the slaves, his death outraged many in Britain and he became known as the 'Demerara Martyr'.

Despite such incidents, some slaves became ministers in their churches, delivering sermons which pointed out the injustices of slavery. Possibly the biggest revolt in the British West Indies occurred in Jamaica, at Christmas in 1831. The rebel leader was a black preacher, Sam Sharpe, head deacon at a Baptist chapel in Montego Bay. The 'Baptist Revolt', as it became known, resulted in the deaths of fourteen white people and caused over a million pounds of damage to property. Again, slave owners took their revenge by killing over five hundred slaves. Sam Sharpe himself was hanged, his final words being: 'I would rather die upon yonder gallows than live in slavery.'

Commenting on the behaviour of the plantation owners, one missionary observed that: 'The most ferocious and savage spirit was manifested... Had I never been in Montego Bay, I must have supposed myself amongst cannibals, or in the midst of the savage hordes of Asia'.

In Britain, the successes and sacrifices of the missionaries were reported back to the congregations that had sent them. As a result, British church-goers took an increased interest in events in the West Indies and in the campaign to free their new converts. The murderous cruelty inflicted on fellow Christians outraged them and it was no coincidence that many of the petitions to abolish slavery and the slave trade originated in churches.

Upon the eventual abolition of slavery, one West Indian hymn expressed the situation from the former slaves' perspective:

> We will be slaves no more,
> Since Christ has made us free,
> Has nailed our tyrants to the cross,
> And brought our liberty.

Full of enthusiasm for this new organisation, Clarkson wrote a shorter version of his essay, *A Summary View of the Slave-Trade and of the Probable Consequences of Its Abolition*, designed to reach a still wider audience than his book. He also set about his researches with increased vigour and set off on a five month tour of Britain. The first destination was Bristol, one of the major centres of the slave trade. As he approached the city on horseback, Clarkson 'began to tremble at the arduous task I had undertaken, of attempting to subvert one of the branches of commerce of the great place ... before me.' He saw the port with its 'hundreds of ships, their masts as thick as they can stand by one another' as visible evidence of the importance of slavery to Bristol. As well as being directly involvement in the transport of slaves, this city was also the port of entry for goods from the West Indies and America, many of which were produced by slaves. It was in Bristol that Clarkson began to interview those involved in the slave trade. By the end of his tour, he had collected the names of over twenty thousand sailors who had sailed on slave ships, along with their reports of what had happened to them. He listened to and recorded the stories of how these men had been recruited in inns and drinking clubs and lured by the promise, often false, of higher wages.

On his visit to Liverpool, another major port deeply involved in the slave trade, Clarkson saw for himself that leg irons and handcuffs were freely available in the city's shops, along with devices for forcing open the jaws of those slaves who refused to eat. The city's connection with slavery was so widespread that one person proposed that 'every brick' in the 'infernal town is cemented with an African's blood.' The idea of abolition was deeply unpopular in Liverpool which was economically dependent on the trade. Even those who had sworn never to sail on a slave ship again were reluctant to speak against the trade in public and anyone who tried to organise a campaign against the slave

A Coffle. Captives were marched, often in yokes, from the inland areas of Africa to the coast for sale to Europeans

Abolitionists employed envelopes like this to convert their friends and business acquaintances. The name was written on the other side

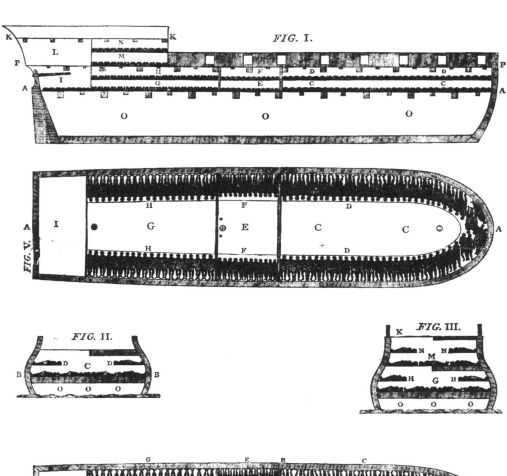

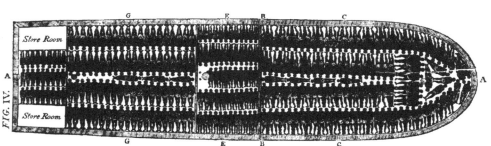

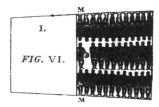

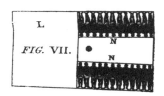

Plan of the 'Brookes'. James Phillips: London, 1789 (1881 d.8.)
The plan demonstrates how slaves were densely
packed into ships for the transatlantic voyage

trade risked being attacked. Clarkson soon came to the notice of some men prepared to use violence to defend the trade. When he tried to charge the officers of one ship with murder for killing a sailor, he was warned that he would be murdered himself. Indeed, the real dangers involved in being an active abolitionist at this time are reflected in the fact that at least one attempt was made on Clarkson's life. Whilst watching a storm on the pier, Clarkson was pushed towards the sea by eight or nine men, including one he had accused of murder. Realising that they intended to throw him into the sea to drown, he: 'darted forward. One of them ... fell down ... and I escaped, not without blows, amidst their ... abuse'.

However, Clarkson was not to be deterred from his cause. With mounting evidence of the corrupt and inhumane practices which the slave trade operated, he set about campaigning in a new way. He suggested that opponents of slavery within a community come together and start local groups. These groups could, he advised, send petitions to Parliament to demand change. The first such petition against slavery had been sent from Bridgwater in 1783, and Clarkson visited the people responsible in order to learn from their experience and to encourage them to continue their campaign. Petitions proved highly popular with the public. Even without the signatures of women, who were prevented from supporting petitions, the petition which Manchester sent to Parliament calling for the regulation of the slave trade contained 10,639 signatures, over a fifth of the city's population.

On Clarkson's return to London, the Committee for Effecting the Abolition of the Slave Trade had thirty members, including the potter and Quaker industrialist Josiah Wedgwood. One of his most memorable contributions to the cause was a design by one of his workers, William Hackwood. Entitled 'Am I Not a Man and a Brother?', it depicted an African slave in chains kneeling with his hands raised to the viewer. This image and slogan were reproduced on a wide variety of goods. Depending on their wealth, men could buy it on gold snuff boxes, while women could wear it on bracelets and hairpins. Clarkson noted that, for once, fashion promoted justice.

By the end of their first year, the Committee had issued 51,432 books and pamphlets and 26,536 copies of reports and other papers. Over a hundred petitions had been sent to Parliament. Issuing pamphlets in an attempt to increase support was nothing new, as the number of people who could read and write was rising rapidly and now included 60% of the adult population. However, in an age when only one in ten men (and no women) could vote, building a mass grass-roots campaign, and demonstrating the support with petitions, was a radical approach to change.

Although dependent on public support, the Committee always had to be careful not to encourage 'mob action'. It was only eight years since the Gordon riots of 1780, when Lord Gordon, a Protestant MP, had led a crowd of fifty thousand to petition Parliament against the lifting of restrictions on Roman Catholics. The riots which broke out lasted a week, hundreds were killed and injured, and up to ten thousand soldiers were needed to restore order. (One of those who had their homes burnt by the mob was Lord Justice Mansfield.) Naturally, with strong Quaker involvement, the Committee would never have considered using violent methods, but the accusation of instigating social unrest could have been very damaging to the cause of abolition.

Even though the Prime Minister, William Pitt, was himself in favour of abolition, Wilberforce knew that it would be a struggle to pass a Parliamentary bill against the slave trade. As so many MPs and peers had a personal financial interest in slavery, the issue split the government. Many people believed that slavery, although difficult to justify on moral grounds, must continue for Britain to become a rich and powerful nation. It was therefore vitally important to establish once and for all that allowing the trade to continue was against Britain's interests as a whole.

In February 1788, Parliament asked the Privy Council's committee for Trade and Plantations to conduct an inquiry into trade with Africa, concentrating especially on the slave trade. Pitt wanted the Privy Council inquiry to be a short one, so that a bill could be moved before the end of the parliamentary session. The Committee had agreed that Clarkson, with the legal assistance of Phillips, should prepare the case for abolition. When the cases were to be heard, those in favour of the trade brought a succession of witnesses to testify as to why the slave trade should be allowed to continue, while the Committee had only a few to argue for its end. Clarkson was particularly dismayed when one man who had promised to support abolition when they met in Liverpool, arrived in London arguing that: 'though the Liberty of Negroes seems now to be the favourite idea, the Liberty of Britons to pursue their lawful Occupations should not be forgotten.' However, despite their far smaller numbers, the Committee's witnesses and Clarkson's detailed research, convinced many that the slave trade should cease.

The Parliamentary debates for and against slavery were conducted by white British men, but we must not forget that black people also spoke out against the trade and tried to persuade others of the moral arguments in favour of abolition. In fact there are a few records of the opinions voiced by the African people living in London. During one debate on the slave trade, John Henry Naimbanna, the son of King Naimbanna of Sierra Leone, who was in London to be educated, heard a pro-slavery witness describe his people in very degrading terms. He was distressed and outraged to hear the speaker's remarks and moved to make an astute and powerful speech:

> If a man should try to kill me, or should sell my family for slaves, he would do an injury to as many as he might kill or sell, but if any one takes away the character of a black people, there is nothing which he may not do to black people ever after. That man, for instance, will beat black men, and say "O, it is only a black man, why should I not beat him" That man will make slaves of black people; for when he has taken away their character, he will say, "O, they are only black people, why should I not make them slaves?" That man will take away all the people of Africa, if he can catch them, and if you ask him, "Why do you take away all those people," he will say "O, they are only black people, they are not like white people, why should not I take them?" That is the reason I cannot forgive the man who takes away the character of the people of my country.

The First Vote in Parliament

Although the abolitionists had gained support, the slave trade won a minor victory when the inquiry took longer than expected and it was too late to introduce a bill in the current session. On the 9th May 1788, the Prime Minister, Pitt, moved that Parliament commit itself to discuss the issue early on in the next session. He stated that until then the matter should not be debated, even though he described it as the most important subject ever raised in the House.

Several abolitionist MPs ignored the Prime Minister's request. As one pointed out, this delay could cost up to ten thousand lives. Charles James Fox, pointed to the pile of petitions and demanded that the 'disgraceful traffic' in slaves be destroyed without delay. The first Parliamentary debate on slavery was under way. When it came to an end, Pitt's resolution was unopposed. It was clear that the abolitionists had won the argument, and the Committee distributed ten thousand copies of the debate to the public.

Within a fortnight, an independent MP, Sir William Dolben, introduced a bill to regulate conditions on board slave ships, which included a restriction on the number of slaves a ship could carry. Another inquiry was set up, with many of the same pro-slavery witnesses brought forward to testify. One witness even suggested that: 'the voyage from the Africa to the West Indies was one of the happiest periods of a Negro's life'! The Committee offered no new witnesses in response. It had no need. Armed with Clarkson's figures, and a report commissioned by Pitt, the arguments that slaves had 'sufficient room, sufficient air, and sufficient provisions' were completely demolished. Even convicts being transported to the penal colonies in Australia had twice as much space on their ships as the slaves.

Even with such compelling evidence, Pitt had to threaten his cabinet with an election before they would support Dolben's bill. It became law on 11th July 1788 and allowed each man just 182cm by 41cm, each woman 152cm by 41cm, each boy 152cm by 36cm and each girl 137cm by 30cm. The bill meant an improvement in conditions but the slaves were still very cramped, especially considering that up to six months would be spent on board the ship.

Although merely improving the lot of slaves on their enforced voyage was not the point of the Committee, Clarkson believed that: 'It was the best bill which could then be obtained'. He complained that: 'The survivors, however their sufferings might have been a little diminished, were reserved for slavery', but it was his expectation that the slave trade would be abolished by Parliament within a year. In fact, it would take another ten years before the slave trade was outlawed and, despite the new restrictions, it was soon making more money than ever before.

'The Print'

Clarkson was still engaged in touring and collecting evidence at an amazing rate. Not only did he conduct interviews personally, but he devised a list of the 145 questions which other supporters could then use to interview more witnesses. On one trip, he was given a plan of a slave ship, showing how the slaves were packed into the cramped space. Clarkson used this idea and drew up'a picture of the Brookes, one of the larger slave ships based in Liverpool. It showed 482 slaves crammed on board, and mentioned how the owners had once somehow managed to fit 609 people into the same space. Published in April 1789, Clarkson's powerful image became known as *The Print* and, still known today, was one of the most effective pieces of propaganda ever produced.

Finally, in April 1789, the Privy Council committee's 850 page report on the slave trade was published. Rather than favouring one side or the other, it simply repeated the testimony of the witnesses, both for and against the trade. As the House of Commons debate on the report was due in less than four weeks, Clarkson prepared the report for use by Wilberforce in Parliament. He divided the material into four parts and each part was summarised by a different person so that Wilberforce could draw upon this evidence during the debate. Clarkson himself wrote the section on his own speciality, the treatment of sailors and African trade.

On 12th May, Wilberforce spoke for three and a half hours in the debate, becoming widely recognised as the leader of the campaign within Parliament. He supported the twelve recommendations put forward by Pitt rather than outright abolition. Yet even this compromise was not good enough for the trade's supporters who insisted on yet another inquiry. Since the abolitionists said they would not call any more witnesses, it was expected that this new hearing would be a short one. However, the slave trade's spokesmen managed once more to extend an inquiry past the end of the Parliamentary session in June, postponing any resolution for yet another year.

Dear friend
Jonathan Peckover. feb. 24 1807

I write to inform you that our Efforts were blessed by Providence last Night in the Promotion of this great Cause of the Abolition of the Slave Trade. I want Words to express the Joy I feel on the Occasion. In favour of the motion there were 283 — against it 16. I shall attend a Committee to-day to deliberate upon some Plan for securing our Victory, when I shall leave London with a Heart full of Gratitude to the Parent of all Mercies, that he has been pleased thus to render a Portion of my life usefull to my oppressed Fellow creatures.

Yours truly
T. Clarkson

Manuscript letter from Thomas Clarkson to Jonathon Peckover (Quaker banker of Wisbech) dated 24 February 1807, expressing the joy Thomas felt at the success, after many difficult years, of the Parliamentary campaign to abolish the slave trade **Wisbech & Fenland Museum**

William Wilberforce by Russell

In Revolutionary France

One of the arguments the pro-slavery lobby used was that if Britain banned the trade, France would take it over. France already had major slave interests, with the Caribbean island of Saint Domingue (now Haiti) alone importing around 18% of all slaves transported from Africa, nearly twice the number imported into the United States. Its soil proved five times as productive as Britain's largest Caribbean island, Jamaica, and enabled the French West Indies to export £9m of goods compared to the British colonies' £5m. Wealth poured into the ports of Bordeaux, Nantes and La Rochelle, just as it did into London, Liverpool and Bristol.

For these reasons, the attitude of the French towards slavery was seen as crucial to the abolitionist cause. A number of French noble patrons had started a campaign against the slave trade, *La Societé des Amis des Noirs*, publishing, among other works, translations of several of Clarkson's works. In order to demonstrate his support for *La Societé*, Clarkson travelled to France in August 1789, shortly after a defining event of the new French Revolution, the storming of the Bastille, on July 14th 1789. He was chosen to be the ambassador for the British Committee because it was considered too dangerous for Wilberforce, a British MP, to visit France. Clarkson, who had already journeyed thousands of miles around Britain was happy to go and commented that: 'As I had no object in view but the good of the cause, it was immaterial to me where I went'.

On his arrival in Calais, he was surprised to see that the country had not fallen into the anarchy reported in the British press. However, he did note that the workings of the old French government had caused much poverty and a large number of beggars. 'If you alighted from your Carriage ... you was instantly attacked. Even on the Road ... a Number of miserable Persons solicited your Charity.' Clarkson felt such scenes proved the benefit of the British system of government, even though he knew of widespread poverty in Britain. Many of the sailors he had interviewed complained that they would starve if they refused to take employment on slave ships.

Despite being a deacon, Clarkson found the sight of people kneeling before religious shrines along the French roadside disturbing. They too appeared to be 'in a state of Slavery' bound by 'superstitious shackles'. It was his hope that recent events in France would lead to a day when 'religion would be kept open to free Enquiry'.

Arriving in Paris, Clarkson drank a dish of coffee (probably produced from coffee beans grown by slaves on Saint Domingue) before exploring the city. The happiness of a people freed from domination was obvious to his eyes. Passing the Bastille, which was still in the process of being demolished, Clarkson asked for a stone as a souvenir of his visit and chose one from a prison cell wall, complete with a carved message from an old prisoner.

The French National Assembly, the French parliament, had just adopted the Declaration of the Rights of Man, with its statement that all men were born, and remained, free and equal. Despite this liberating declaration of equality, the issue of ending the slave trade, never mind abolishing slavery entirely, was just as controversial in France as it was in Britain. One of the members of *La Societé* calculated that only a quarter of the National Assembly's 1,200 members would vote against slavery. It appeared that only if the British Parliament ended the slave trade first would the French follow. Unfortunately, this situation was mirrored in reverse in Britain, where some MPs would only vote against the trade if the French had already done so.

Just as today, France's colonies had direct representatives in the French parliament and during his visit, Clarkson met six men from the 'coloured' (mixed race) population of Saint Domingue. They were not slaves, but neither did they have equal rights with the white population. These men were in Paris to demand representation for the coloured population in the Assembly, but pressure from the white slave owners meant their calls were ignored. Desperate to see justice done, their leader told Clarkson that if peaceful means failed: 'We can produce as good soldiers on our estates as those in France. Our own arms shall make us independent and respectable'. Clarkson advised patience, but was right in his forecast of what would happen if they were not treated fairly: 'If the planters should persevere in their intrigue, and the National Assembly in delay, a fire would be lighted up in [St Domingue] which would not easily be extinguished'. Only three months later, one of the men whom he had met led an unsuccessful rebellion in the colony and was brutally executed.

At the other end of the social scale, Louis XVI, still then King of France but with few remaining powers, was presented with copies of Clarkson's books. Despite the fact that France had promoted this appalling practice of transporting human cargo for great profit, it was thought that a copy of 'The Print' was too horrifying for the King to see.

Clarkson left France in February of 1790. One of the leaders of *La Societé* described his parting message on the prospects of the abolition of the slave trade in both countries: 'He hoped the day was near at hand, when two great nations, which had been hitherto distinguished only for their hostility would unite in so sublime a measure; and that they would follow up their union by another, still more lovely, for the preservation of eternal and universal peace'. Sadly Clarkson's vision did not materialise, the two countries would soon be at war and his support for the ideals of the French Revolution would be unpopular with many.

Saint Domingue

The rebellion of 1789 in Saint Domingue was to be one of many, as the black population of this colony sought to claim the grand ideals of France's revolution - 'Liberty, Equality and Brotherhood' - for themselves. In the 1780's the coloured class of Saint Domingue was growing in power and capital and aspired to the equal rights denied to them by France and the white elite. This class became increasingly restless and it was inevitable that their own message of revolution would be passed down to the slaves. Indeed, although this was the most profitable colony for the white plantation owners who built elegant residences and lived a decadent life-style, it had the highest mortality rate amongst the slaves.

It was Bookman, a runaway slave who crossed from Jamaica to Saint Domingue who first spread the call for rebellion across the black slave population of the island. With nothing to lose, these mainly first generation slaves with memories of a free life in Africa were quick to respond to the call to revolt. In 1791 there was a major slave rebellion. Hundreds of plantations were destroyed and up to twenty thousand slaves escaped to live in the jungles and hills. Bookman was captured by the French, but the slaves had found their most famous leader, Toussaint L'Ouverture, the grandson of an African King who had been captured in battle and sold to a Portuguese slave trader. L'Ouverture worked as a domestic slave but was never truly subjugated by slavery, declaring: 'I was born a slave, but nature gave me the soul of a free man'.

With France and Britain at war, L'Ouverture seized his chance in August 1793 and led a rebellion against France in the name of justice: 'I have undertaken vengeance. I want liberty and equality to reign'. The British invaded the colony, with the dual aim of seizing it as part of their empire and stopping the rebellion spreading to their existing possessions. However, the British were surprised by the effective resistance from former slaves and their forces were further weakened by disease. L'Ouverture was able successfully to negotiate a truce: if the British left him in peace, he would not attack Jamaica. After years of struggle with France and England and between different groups on the island, Toussaint L'Ouverture managed to unite the island, give the colony a new constitution and make himself Governor General of Haiti.

Toussaint worked hard to restore the economy and social order in Saint Domingue from 1800 to 1802, but his success was short-lived. When Napoleon Bonaparte became France's leader, he sent his brother-in-law with another army to recapture the colony. This time L'Ouverture was defeated by deceit and taken to France, proclaiming: 'In overthrowing me you have cut down in Saint Domingue only the trunk of the tree of liberty. It will spring up again by the roots, for they are numerous and deep'.

He was proved right. Although L'Ouverture died imprisoned in the cold French Alps in April 1803, after further revolts, the colony he had first ruled in freedom became the independent state of Haiti in 1804, the first free nation in the region.

Unfortunately, this was not the end of the colony's problems. A civil war followed the murder of Jean Jacques Dessalines, 'Emperor Jacques I of Hayti', one of the leaders of the revolt. The colony divided into two. The commander of the army, Henry Christophe, controlled the north of the country as King Henry, whilst a rival set himself up as president of a republic in the south.

Henry I proved to be a good ruler if not a good democrat. He was determined to demonstrate the equality of Haitians to Europeans, and created a monarchy and aristocracy on the island. It was his aim to equal the splendour and the glory which Europe had enjoyed for too long at the expense of African slaves. He built the magnificent Citadel with the bricks of old plantation houses and set about restoring the country's wealth and breaking up the large plantations. This proved a very difficult task as France continued to lay claim on her former colony and consequently no other nation would recognise the new state, and most refused to trade with it. The export of coffee halved and the country's trade in sugar collapsed completely.

In 1814, Henry wrote to both Wilberforce and Clarkson for help and advice. While the former was more concerned with the prospects of converting the country's people to Protestantism, Clarkson showed 'genuine excitement and sincerity in setting about obtaining a public recognition of complete equality for the Haitians' and became the King's adviser in Europe. Together, they organised for schools and a Royal College to be founded, and took other measures to reform the Society. In 1819, Henry asked if Clarkson would formally become his ambassador to France, an honour he had to decline. Even so, Clarkson continued to talk to the French government about the situation between the two countries and established that France would not try to recapture her colony by force.

In 1820, Henry was left half-paralysed after a fit. When his army deserted, he shot himself. Although his sons were killed by the army, his wife and two daughters were allowed to live in exile because of their succession of good deeds for the poor. They stayed with Clarkson for several months whilst looking for a permanent home in Britain. One evening, they were invited to dine with Wilberforce, who was writing a letter to a friend as they arrived: 'Dinner is just going on the table with an ex-Queen and 2 Ex-Princesses with others of inferior note for guests'.

Back in Haiti, another civil war followed and the two halves of the country were reunited under the control of the south. The Haitian people abandoned both palaces and plantations and returned to a simpler agricultural life, but mismanagement of resources led to poverty for all but a small elite. Sadly, this is a situation which continues to this day. Even though the slaves of Haiti had successfully revolted against their oppressed state with great courage and might, they had not been able to secure a future of equality and justice for the coming generations.

On Clarkson's return from France, the House of Commons inquiry was still interviewing pro-slave trade witnesses. One of the main issues of dispute was exactly how the slaves were obtained in Africa. At one time, the British Royal African Company (founded in 1663 with the support of Charles II) had a monopoly on the supply of slaves from areas of British influence. It had built several large forts on the coast, some of which remain today, where slaves would be held securely underground before being loaded on board ships for transportation to the New World. With the explosion in demand for African slaves in the Eighteenth Century, private companies took over this trade. They showed higher profits largely because they did not have to bear the high cost of maintaining such permanent settlements, nor replace the casualties of a variety of African diseases which proved fatal to Europeans. Since the geography of the West African coastline afforded few usable ports, slave ships would anchor off the coast then send in small canoes and boats to collect their human cargo. As there were no longer large quantities of slaves waiting to be collected, the ships might spend months off the coast, slowly filling up before setting sail for the Americas.

The slavers testifying before the inquiry said that the slaves were purchased at markets run by Africans. In some cases this was true, but Clarkson wanted to show that this was not the whole story. He had heard of a British sailor who had been on one of the canoes and wanted this man to act as a witness. The problem was that the only thing known about the sailor was that he was now in the navy on a ship being repaired. No-one knew his name, his rank or even which ship he was on. It was typical of Clarkson's dedication and determination that he set off on a three week tour of the Royal Dockyards to find this man. Starting in Deptford, he went along the Thames to Woolwich, Chatham and Sheerness, before heading to Portsmouth and finally Plymouth. He boarded 317 ships to interview their crews before finally finding the witness, Isaac Parker, who confirmed that he had seen villages attacked and people enslaved directly by the ships' crews.

The Committee was now faced with an uncomfortable choice. They could either accept another year's delay as the inquiry continued past the deadline for introducing a new bill that year, or leave unanswered several new points raised by the slave traders. Wilberforce advised the former. Again, those in favour of the slave trade had managed to avoid a vote.

Slavery was still a major issue in the country, but subscriptions to the Committee were down on the previous two years. Clarkson was also finding it increasingly difficult to discover people with personal experience of the trade prepared to give evidence against it. One problem was that many civil servants knew that the government was divided over the issue of slavery and did not wish to commit themselves publicly to one side or the other until they were sure which side would win, as they were afraid it would affect their careers. Another problem was that some people were intimidated by Clarkson actually writing down their answers to his questions, so sometimes he had to remember everything they said and then write it down later.

On yet another of Clarkson's tours, this one taking him seven thousand miles around the north of England, he found only twenty new witnesses. Although disappointed, as he had hoped for a hundred, Clarkson was already responsible for over two thousand pages of testimony being given to Parliament.

The House of Commons inquiry continued into 1791. After the Committee arranged for every MP to have a summary of the evidence given, Wilberforce moved a bill to abolish the slave trade on 18th April. The debate went on late into the night, and when the vote came at 3:30am the next morning, the bill was defeated by 163 votes to 88. Although they had hoped for victory, the Committee was not surprised by this set-back. Parliament was filled with, and only elected by, the wealthy. The French Revolution had frightened this group since if the French poor could overthrow the state, then why not the poor in Britain? In March of this year, Thomas Paine had published the second part of his book, *The Rights of Man*, praising the French revolutionaries and denouncing the British monarchy. With his call for equality in property and liberty, Paine was soon accused of treason and was forced into exile.

Clarkson knew that his summary of the evidence on the slave trade and its implications for slave-owners was: 'considered by many [MPs] as poisonous as that of the Rights of Man'. Nevertheless, he continued to support both abolition and the Revolution, which he believed had created: 'a great Nation free and happy'. He attended a dinner on 14th July to mark the second anniversary of the storming of the Bastille, much to the distress of some of his friends including Wilberforce who commented that: 'He could not have done a more mischievous thing to the cause'. When the two met in Staffordshire later in the year, Clarkson noted that: 'almost the first word Mr Wilberforce said to me was this: "O Clarkson, I wanted much to see you to tell you to keep clear from the subject of the French Revolution and I hope you will."' Clarkson did keep quiet in the company of those who disapproved strongly, but he could never quite see why people who supported one of his causes would not also support the other. 'I shou'd think it quite consistent with an enemy to Slavery to rejoice in the French having acquir'd liberty,' he told a friend.

In 1663 Charles II chartered a royal company with a monopoly of African trade, chiefly in slaves

A medal struck "In commemoration of the extinction of colonial slavery throughout the British Dominions in the reign of William IV on August 1, 1834." The reverse shows a freed man standing in sunlight holding broken chains: "This is the Lord's Doing: It is marvellous in our eyes. Psalm 118 v. 23 JUBILEE AUGT 1834." After partially ending slavery in 1834, Parliament finally terminated slavery throughout British colonies in 1838. Thereafter, abolition became a key factor in that cultural imperialism which became the hallmark of the British for a century or more.

The "guinea", struck at the order of Charles II to publicise his new company, was named after the West African area that produced the coin's high-quality gold

Raffish Charles Fox was a valuable recruit to abolition. He had only to wave his wand, Pitt said, to charm the House

Freetown, Sierra Leone (1792) painted by John Beckett to record for John Clarkson the progress made by the settlement in its eight months of existence. Clarkson had escorted twelve hundred American slaves back to Africa and was their first governor under the Sierra Leone Company

Sierra Leone

One of Clarkson's strongest convictions was that Britain would make more money from trading fairly with Africa, than it did by enslaving its population. From the start of his investigations, he collected a wide range of African-made goods to demonstrate that its people were far from the ignorant savages slavers made them out to be.

In 1787 Granville Sharp had founded the Province of Freedom, now known as Freetown, as a haven for freed slaves who wished to return to Africa. Situated on the shore of St George's Bay, the world's third largest natural harbour, this was clearly an ideal location to set up a trading centre. Although the first settlement was destroyed in 1790 during conflict between an African chief and local slavers, Sharp had organised a group of British businessmen to trade with the Province. These men sent some relief supplies to the settlers in order to help them survive and rebuild the settlement, but could not fully develop trade without becoming a company.

The Sierra Leone Company received its company charter from Parliament in 1791. Its directors, elected by the shareholders, included both Clarkson and Wilberforce and it was suggested that some other MPs supported this company dedicated to help former slaves because they were embarrassed by their voting in favour of the slave trade in April.

When some of the original shareholders, recruited from the abolition campaign and sympathetic bankers and merchants, began selling some of their shares there were fears that slavers would take the venture over. As part of the plan to stop this happening and attract other businessmen, the settlement lost some of its independence and was run from London, rather than Sierra Leone. Clarkson claimed that: 'No Country affords a finer Prospect to the Merchant.' His younger brother, John, was sent to Nova Scotia, Canada, to arrange for the passage of over a thousand Africans to Sierra Leone. Many had fought with the British armies during the American War of Independence, and had been moved to Nova Scotia by the British after their defeat in that war.

John Clarkson spent over a year in Sierra Leone as governor, always writing to his brother Thomas on its progress. John's message to these free people of Africa when he left made plain his hopes for their future: 'God only knows how much I feel for your prosperity and the happiness of this vast Continent'. In reply, they hoped that he would return, so that they could 'see you with our Longing Eyes'.

The Sierra Leone Company was dissolved with the end of the slave trade and the colony given over to Britain to rule. To encourage its success, in 1814 Thomas Clarkson became a chairman of the 'Society for the Encouraging the Black Settlers at Sierra Leone, and the Natives of Africa generally, in the Cultivation of their Soil, by the Sale of their Produce'. This organisation established trade between Britain and Sierra Leone, making this settlement one of the first examples of fair trade between Britain and Africa. By 1850, over 50,000 freed slaves had returned to Africa to live in Sierra Leone. It became the first British colony in Africa, before winning independence in 1961.

Death of Capt. Ferrer, the captain of the Armistad in July 1839, from J.W. Barber, A History of the Armistad Captives, 1840. The Armistad was taking slaves between ports in Cuba when it was seized by captives who tried to return to Africa

The Outbreak of War

As was his habit of a lifetime, Clarkson once again set off on another tour of Britain. He knew that it was important to help raise morale after the defeat in Parliament, of what he had personally witnessed to be: 'the enthusiasm of the nation [against the slave trade] at this time'. The opposition to his campaign was still there, but was clearly outnumbered in the country at the grass-roots level: 'Great pains were taken by interested persons in many places to prevent public meetings. But no efforts could avail'.

On this tour, Clarkson was keen to promote the idea that people could show their opposition to the slave trade by not buying the goods produced by slaves, such as West Indian sugar and rum. Today, such action would be called a consumer boycott, but this was almost a century before this strategy would be named after a protest against a landlord's agent, Charles Boycott, in Ireland. Today we can observe that Clarkson's genius in organising the abolition campaign was his willingness to adapt and publicise the ideas of others. Mass petitions to Parliament was one example, 'The Print' of slaves packed on board a ship another, the boycott a third.

Early in 1791, Clarkson read a pamphlet by William Fox of London, *An Address to the People of Great Britain*, suggesting a boycott, and immediately started to have it reprinted and distributed. This practice would hit not only the slave-owners, but also the government through loss of tax revenue. It soon gained popular support, up to five hundred families gave up sugar after reading the pamphlet in one area and Clarkson calculated that one less slave would be brought to the West Indies for every two families who joined the boycott. Some people switched to honey as a sweetener, some insisted on sugar from the East Indies produced without slave labour, others adopted maple syrup. Clarkson was proud to note that: 'There was no town, through which I passed, in which there was not some one individual who had left off the use of sugar... Even children ... excluded with the most virtuous resolution, the sweets ... from their lips'. One London grocer reported that the demand for sugar had fallen by a third, while one in Birmingham said sales had halved within four months. Clarkson estimated that 300,000 people joined the boycott at some point.

Unfortunately the boycott of sugar did not have the effect on slavery that he had hoped, partly because the effect of falling demand was drowned out by rising prices as the rebellion in San Domingue badly hit that island's exports. Another obstacle was that the boycott never had the full support of the Committee. Wilberforce disapproved of the idea and it was not until 1795, four years after Clarkson personally started promoting boycotts, that the Committee said 'a decided preference' should be given to alternatives to slave-produced goods.

There was far more agreement on the need for petitions. In order to achieve maximum impact, Clarkson suggested that they should arrive just before Wilberforce moved another motion for the abolition of the slave trade in April 1792. A record total of 519 petitions poured in, with one arriving just minutes before the debate started. This time, Manchester's petition was signed by around twenty thousand men, while Glasgow's and Edinburgh's petitions carried a total of twenty two thousand signatures. In contrast, the supporters of the slave trade managed just four petitions, with one addition suggesting the trade be reformed rather than abolished.

Wilberforce started his speech at 6pm and the debate once more carried on long into the night, with the last speech, from Prime Minister Pitt, finishing at 6am the next morning. Clarkson had tipped a House of Commons door-keeper ten guineas (£10.50, a significant sum then) to admit thirty supporters of the motion to watch the debate. He did not witness it himself and so missed Wilberforce praising him as a: 'Gentleman whose services in the whole of this great cause can never be over rated'. He also missed opponents of the motion calling him an 'itinerant clergyman' who 'extorted signatures from the sick, the indigent and the traveller'.

Towards the end of the debate, a government minister proposed to add a single word to the motion. Rather than commit Parliament to abolish the British slave trade, he suggested it decide to abolish it gradually. Moderation should be the rule, he said. This argument satisfied no-one. Pro-slavery MPs were reluctant to have any commitment to end the trade, even though with their proven skill in dragging out proceedings they believed that the end could be delayed for years. Abolitionists argued that if something was wrong, then it should be stopped immediately, not at some vague time in the future. One MP, Charles James Fox, asked, 'How can you carry on the slave trade moderately? How can a country be pillaged and destroyed in moderation? We cannot modify injustice. The question is to what period we shall prolong it'.

Parliamentary procedure means that votes on amendments such as this are taken first. Passing it would mean MPs would then be faced with the choice of gradual abolition or doing nothing. Seeing this as a better option than allowing a vote on immediate abolition, the pro-slave trade MPs ensured the amendment was passed. Supporters of abolition were now faced with a dilemma. Was a little better than nothing? If they voted in favour and the motion was passed, it would be extremely difficult to persuade Parliament to hurry up proceedings and the trade would continue for years. If they voted against, saying it was not good enough, they could be accused of not really wanting to abolish the trade at all. In the end, the vote was 230 votes in favour of gradual abolition, 85 against. After some further debate, the date for abolition was fixed as 1796, four years away.

Once a Bill has been passed by the Commons, it must then be passed by the House of Lords before it can become law. Politically, the Lords was then a more important place than it is today. Nowadays it revises bills and can delay their passage for a year, but in the end it cannot stop laws the House of Commons has passed. The Lords then was much more of an equal partner, fully able and willing to reject measures which had the support of the Commons. This was the first time the issue slavery had been debated in the Lords, so there was yet another inquiry into the trade. Again, it continued past the end of a Parliamentary session, postponing any vote for another year.

Once more, Clarkson embarked on the search for witnesses for an inquiry. Added to his previous problems was that fact that ship owners, with the threat of future abolition hanging over their trade, were trying to make as much money as possible. Hardly anyone with experience of the trade could be found in Britain as three times the usual number of ships joined the trade. The House of Commons vote had made things worse, not better, for Africans.

Later in 1792, the French royal family were taken prisoner by the revolutionaries and Russia and Prussia declared war on France. The National Assembly which had run France was replaced by a Convention. One of its first acts was to confer French citizenship on, among others, Clarkson and Wilberforce. As a Tory, Wilberforce was not happy with this and demonstrated his support for the old regime by attending meetings to raise funds for those who had fled France. Clarkson accepted the honour and may have visited France once more at this time, seeing the 'Excellent Republic will be established on ye Ruins of Despotism & arbitrary Power' which he described to a friend.

Despite his personal beliefs, Clarkson realised that support for the new government of France was not popular in Britain, particularly after the execution of Louis XVI in January 1793. Indeed, France declared war on Britain less than a fortnight later and the two countries would be at war for most of the following twenty-two years. As a reaction, Britain passed the Aliens Act, stopping foreigners from entering the country.

The Lowest Point

In Spring of 1793 Clarkson was also dismayed when a motion for the House of Commons to reopen the issue of abolition failed. Moreover, a new bill to stop British merchants sending slaves to foreign markets was only narrowly defeated in June of this year. With the outbreak of war, MPs had other things on their minds than slavery and campaigners for both sides of the abolition issue found it difficult to persuade them to attend the vote.

In the House of Lords, opposition to Wilberforce's bill was led by the Duke of Clarence, the third son of King George III. He had served in the navy and had visited the Caribbean. When he returned to Britain, he wrote to friends that slaves lived: 'in a condition of humble happiness'. Clarkson noted that the Duke was 'so miserable an orator that it is a disadvantage to any cause he supports'. Even so, he succeeded in delaying the bill for another year and attacked abolitionists as: 'either fanatics or hypocrites, and in one of those classes I rank Mr Wilberforce'.

His exertions over the past seven years caused major strain on Clarkson's physical and mental health and he was suffering from nervous exhaustion. He knew it would take at least three years before the British slave trade would come to an end and he was worried that he might not even survive that long. 'My mind has been literally bent like a Bow to one gloomy subject,' he wrote to a friend. 'The Anxiety ... the Mental and Bodily Labour connected with it, the vexations, disappointments ... have contributed to make inroads in my Constitution. I feel myself too almost daily getting worse & worse.'

Clarkson was also faced with financial problems, having spent around £1,500, over half his wealth, in support of the cause. He had personally paid for 'whole coaches full' of witnesses to travel to London and for their lodgings while in the capital. Others had received a financial allowance from the Committee, but had complained about its inadequacy, so Clarkson had given them more money himself. Two of his witnesses, a surgeon and his assistant on a slave ship, had seen the captain brutally murder a 15 year-old slave girl. Wilberforce had mentioned the case in the House of Commons debate the previous year and the captain was then tried for murder. To everyone's surprise, he was acquitted, and the two witnesses were then tried for perjury, as it was said they had lied when giving evidence against the captain. Both blamed Clarkson for their situation and repeatedly asked him for money, only stopping when he found one man a job in Sierra Leone and raised £100 for the other to emigrate to America. He had always given generously to those who asked, 'lest the Cause suffer', even though he knew that not everyone offering help was 'actuated by pure motives' and that some sought only money or social advancement.

Even after he sold his shares in the Sierra Leone Company, Clarkson reckoned that he had just enough left to retire into an 'obscure Life'. Carrying on as before would lead to financial ruin and an early death. He wondered whether people would hate him for giving up the cause, and whether he would be able to live with the decision himself. The Archdeacon of Lichfield and Coventry, an honorary member of the Committee, met Clarkson and was worried about the possibility of his retirement. He went as far as to say that: 'If he retired, the cause was absolutely lost'. The Archdeacon acknowledged that Wilberforce knew more about slavery than anyone in Parliament, 'yet his knowledge is as nothing compared to Mr Clarkson's, who is the link by which it is all managed'. In the end, an appeal was launched to raise funds for Clarkson's work. Some people felt he was a little selfish in his efforts to attract subscribers to the appeal, but for once Clarkson was simply working as hard for himself as he had for others over the years.

The fund-raising was not made any easier by Clarkson's known views on the situation in France. Anyone who was not open in their support for the King was accused of being a Jacobin (a revolutionary republican, named after the hall of the Jacobin Friars in Paris in which meetings took place) and risked prosecution under new treason and sedition laws which had been rushed through Parliament. The swift passage of these laws was in complete contrast to the slow speed of the anti-slavery legislation. Several of the Committee's supporters had already been charged with treason, including one of the organisers of the Manchester petitions, Thomas Walker. Clarkson visited Walker to offer his support. He wrote: 'I have no business in Manchester, but wishing to see you,' although typically of Clarkson, he also wished to discuss some 'points which may be useful to the Cause to ascertain'.

As a supporter of the reform of Parliament, Walker's house had been attacked by a mob four times and on the most recent occasion, he had been seen with six friends carrying guns to protect themselves. For this action, they were accused of 'attempting .. with force of arms' to overthrow the government, but after an expensive trial were acquitted. More trials of supporters of constitutional reform followed in London, but these also resulted in acquittals. Had they been found guilty, Clarkson would have emigrated in despair: 'for if it was look'd upon to be treason to belong to such popular Societies as the constitutional Society... no one was safe'.

In this highly-charged political atmosphere, the work of the Committee effectively stopped. Another bill passed the House of Commons in 1794, but was ignored by the House of Lords, along with all other previous measures. The only high point was the abolition of slavery in France's colonies, passed by the French Convention in 1794. In part, however, this was a response to Britain's campaign to capture the French West Indies. The French hoped that their former slaves would fight rather than accept the return to slavery which the British re-imposed whenever they captured an island. Parliament meanwhile shifted the deadline for abolition to 'not before the end of the war with France'.

The following year, Parliament passed the Seditious Practices Act. It banned any criticism of the King or Parliament, as well as all public gatherings of more than fifty people. It was impossible to run an effective campaign under such conditions. The Committee met just six times from 1795 to 1797, then adjourned proceedings indefinitely. The British slave trade, which at one point Parliament had resolved would be finished by 1796, was continuing as strongly as ever. The anti-slavery cause stood at its lowest point for years.

Life with Family and Friends

Although a serious set-back to the cause, the break was exactly what Clarkson needed to recover his health. On his travels around Britain for the cause, he often stayed with a Quaker friend near Penrith on the edge of the Lake District. The landscape enchanted him and in 1794 he spent most of his remaining money buying 35 acres on the shore of Ullswater where he built a cottage. To their surprise, friends noted that he would talk of little else but his new cottage, and that they now had to persuade him to talk about the cause of abolition. The subject of finding a wife was also discussed as Clarkson resolved to marry not long after his new cottage was built. Friends expected him to marry Catherine Buck, 'a very amiable & sensible young Lady', whom Clarkson had met some years ago whilst in Bury St Edmunds, but he refused to confirm that she would be his bride. He had, in fact, discussed the prospects of marriage with Catherine's father, but was worried that he would be too poor to be acceptable.

Clarkson finally proposed marriage in May 1795 and the two were married in Catherine's local church in Bury St Edmunds in January 1796. It was clear to all that Clarkson and Catherine were highly suited to each other. He strongly believed that women were the intellectual equals of men and attacked the way that 'homage is paid to their beauty, very little is paid to their opinions'. Catherine certainly had opinions, supporting, like Clarkson, the aims of the French Revolution. The couple arrived in Ullswater in the spring and by October Clarkson was writing to Catherine's father to tell how: 'my dearest Catherine was this morning delivered of a fine Boy & that both She and the Infant are well'. They named their son Thomas.

A succession of visitors to the family noted how Clarkson had thrown himself into life there. He grew a variety of crops, from wheat to turnips, and kept birds, sheep and bullocks, taking them to Penrith market to sell. One observed that: 'He sums up the evidence for & against his hen-pens, his duck crews & goose house & its convenience with the same detail & precision he sum'd up the evidence on the Slave trade'. Indeed, just as he had kept records of his researches into the slave trade, Clarkson kept a 'most regular & minute journal' of his farm. He was clearly entranced by his new life, by 'The bud and the blossom, the rising and the falling leaf, the blade of corn and the ear, the seed-time and the harvest, the sun that warms and ripens, the cloud that cools, and emits the fruitful shower – these and a hundred objects afford daily food for the religious growth of the mind'.

Catherine, too, was enjoying her new home. 'My life here suits me exactly... It is regular & tranquil. My Husband enjoys good Health & spirits. My little Boy is ye sweetest fellow you ever saw. Every thing about us is improving & flourishing,' she wrote to her parents.

The Lake District was becoming a popular location. In 1799, the poets Wordsworth and Coleridge took up residence with their families. The Clarksons got on well with both and they were soon making regular visits to and from each other's homes. William Wordsworth shared much of Clarkson's history, both having studied at St John's College, Cambridge with the intention of becoming a clergyman, before choosing another career. Similarly, Catherine became a close friend of Dorothy Wordsworth, William's sister. Samuel Taylor Coleridge was another regular visitor who particularly appreciated Catherine's warmth.

However, Coleridge was to be less appreciative of Clarkson's advice on the subject of starting up a weekly magazine. He was asked to help find some subscribers, but instead devoted himself to the matter and presented Coleridge with a virtually complete business plan, most of which he ignored. 'He never has more than one thought in his brain at a time, let it be great or small,' Coleridge wrote to a friend. 'I have called him the moral Steam-Engine, or the Giant with one idea – Heaven knows! How well I love and how very highly I revere him. He shall be my Friend, Exemplar, Saint – any thing, only not my Counsellor in matters of Business.' Despite his assertion, Clarkson's advice was typically sound and if Coleridge had followed it, it is likely that his magazine would have been more of a success than it turned out to be.

The Clarksons' son also proved popular with their literary friends. The children's author Mary Lamb is said to have written *Tales from Shakespeare* for the young Tom Clarkson and she often enquired after his health, as his appreciation of 'my first production was one of the things I built on'. Years later, when Tom Clarkson was thinking of leaving Cambridge University without completing his degree, William Wordsworth wrote to him: 'Know thyself, look into the goodly garden of thy own mind, and pluck up the weeds... Bestir thyself and be a Son worthy of thy never to be forgotten Father'.

In 1803, a liver problem meant that Catherine spent much of the year in Clifton and Bury St Edmunds, undergoing medical care. As she was advised not to return to the colder climate of Ullswater, Clarkson reluctantly sold the land and his cottage to live with his wife in Bury St Edmunds. Most of his spare time was spent writing a book on the Quakers, published in 1806. It was the first attempt by someone outside the Society of Friends, as the Quakers call themselves, to sympathetically explain their beliefs. Dorothy Wordsworth wrote to congratulate him on the book and the £600 it had earned him: 'We may now fairly call you rich people,' she said, before comparing them with her brother's fortunes: 'Alas! poetry is a bad trade... and William's works sell slowly'.

Long years working with many members of the Society of Friends had led Clarkson to appreciate their faith and the way they led their lives. When asked by the Russian Emperor some years later whether he was a Quaker himself, Clarkson replied that: 'I am not so in name, but I hope in spirit, I am nine-tenths of their way in spirit'. The admiration was mutual, and Clarkson's *The Print* was one of the handful of pictures Quakers were allowed to display in their homes. In particular, Clarkson strongly admired the habits of Quaker women, whom he saw as 'rational, useful and dignified', and the equal treatment they enjoyed, uniquely able to become ministers in their church. Women ministers, Clarkson thought, represented a 'new era in female history'.

The Campaign Resumes

In 1801 Ireland had become part of the United Kingdom and was represented in the House of Commons by a hundred MPs, few of whom had any personal or constituency interest in the slave trade. Indeed, the political situation in both Britain and France had changed significantly since 1797, although the war between the two countries still continued. As part of the war campaign, Britain had seized most of France's colonies in the West Indies and had re-imposed slavery; this meant that no-one could now suggest that if Britain stopped the slave trade France would take it over.

France herself now had another absolute ruler, the Emperor Napoleon Bonaparte. Although his undoubted skills made France more of a military threat to Britain, she was now seen as less of a political threat to the British establishment than a democracy run by the people. In 1802, Napoleon had restored slavery in the few French colonies left, further reducing his appeal to those in Britain who wanted political change.

A new era in the work of the Committee had begun with the resumption of its business in May 1804, with the refreshed Clarkson again playing a leading role. Another bill to abolish the slave trade was introduced to the House of Commons by Wilberforce at the end of May 1804 and was quickly passed. It then passed to the House of Lords at the end of June. The Committee's main adviser in this House was Lord Grenville who suggested that, once again, the end of the parliamentary session was too close to allow the bill to pass and that if they tried to force a vote, it would be defeated. It was agreed to try again the following year.

When the bill was re-introduced in 1805, it was defeated in the Commons by just seven votes. Wilberforce and Clarkson blamed their own complacency in assuming that a measure which had easily been passed the previous year would have no trouble in being reaffirmed. Consequently, the abolition campaign had put too little effort into reminding its supporters to vote, unlike its opponents who made sure that every MP who would vote against was present. From looking at the voting lists Clarkson realised that nine MPs who had always previously voted for abolition had been absent this time. He also knew that they were sorry for this absence and now sat 'on the Stool of Repentance', aware of the consequences of their actions. Most of the Irish MPs also missed the vote, so Clarkson was confident that with a little more diligence concerning attendance, the bill would be passed in 1806. 'It was now almost certain, to the inexpressible joy of the committee, that the cause ... could be carried in the next session,' Clarkson later wrote. One small gain for the cause was an Order of the Privy Council (an important unelected committee which advises the sovereign) banning the re-introduction of slavery in captured colonies.

Clarkson embarked on another tour of Britain, reporting back that previous supporters were still 'faithful' to the cause, but also that many young people did not remember the debates and the surrounding publicity of a decade ago. Based on the evidence he had collected, Clarkson published a new pamphlet on the behaviour and effects of slave-holders in Africa. His visits were also important in revitalising the work of several local abolition committees.

Shortly after Clarkson's return to London, the Prime Minister, William Pitt, died. Although one of the original friends of the cause, he had recently been forced by splits in his government to be, at best, neutral over the issue. The new Prime Minister was Lord Grenville, a friend to the abolition cause, and Charles James Fox, another strong abolition supporter, was his Foreign Secretary. 'We have rather more friends in the Cabinet than formerly', Clarkson wrote in a news-letter to supporters, urging a 'spontaneous' lobby of MPs when abolition was next discussed.

The first major step towards humane practice came with a new government bill confirming the 1805 Order of Council. It passed both Houses of Parliament and received royal assent in May. Clarkson estimated that this measure alone would save 35,000 people 'from being annually torn from their Country'. The next step came when Grenville put forward a resolution that the African slave trade was: 'contrary to the principles of justice, humanity and policy' and that steps should be taken to abolish it. This passed the Commons by 114 votes to 15 and then the Lords by 41 votes to 20. It was the first occasion on which the Lords had condemned the slave trade. Two further measures were also passed in the rush of activity. On the request of Wilberforce, Parliament asked King George III to negotiate with other countries to end the slave trade. Finally in July, a bill stopping new ships from joining the slave trade became law. Along with the rest of the Committee, Clarkson was delighted with the progress that had been made commenting that: 'It is 'universally believed … that the Slave-trade had received its death-wound'.

However, the trade had yet to be actually abolished. Success appeared to have been just around the corner, but before Parliament resumed Lord Grenville's coalition government lost one of its leading figures and supporters of abolition with the death of Charles James Fox. Seeking public support, Grenville called a general election in October.

Before the great Reform Acts later in the Nineteenth Century, British general elections were curious affairs and the result could never be predicted with any certainty. The right to vote was based largely on wealth and property ownership and just one man in ten, and no women, could vote. Yet more wealth was needed before a man was eligible to become an MP. Voting itself was conducted publicly, rather than in secret, leading to widespread bribery and intimidation. In some cases the parties themselves arranged that they would not fight a seat and the voters had no say at all in the outcome.

As today, each MP had a constituency, the area they represent in the House of Commons. Today, the country is divided into over 650 areas with roughly equal numbers of voters, each of which returns one MP. In Clarkson's day, there were two sorts of constituencies, borough (town) seats and county seats. The borough seats had been allocated to towns years ago and were now completely out of date. Several large new cities had no MPs at all, while other constituencies, the so-called rotten or pocket boroughs (because they were 'in the pocket of' a local landowner who had power to decide who would be MP), had declined to just a handful of electors. One such borough had eight landowners whose votes returned two MPs for a constituency which had not a single person living in it. Every other part of Britain was covered by the county MPs, with each county having two MPs. Again, there were significant differences in size with the smallest county, Rutland, having only six hundred voters.

In contrast, Wilberforce's constituency of Yorkshire was the largest of them all, with twenty thousand electors covering many miles. Wilberforce was in the process of writing a pamphlet, a *Letter on the Abolition of the Slave Trade Addressed to the Freeholders* [the voters] *and Other Inhabitants of Yorkshire*, when the election was called. It was the first public statement Wilberforce had made to his voters against slavery, although he had been involved in the campaign for over twenty years. Part of the reason for his earlier silence was that the other Yorkshire MP, Henry Lascelles, was both a fellow supporter of Pitt and a slave owner. The two men could work together on just about every issue but the slave trade, and Wilberforce was reluctant to disrupt their relationship by making it an election issue. Indeed, Yorkshire usually returned its two MPs without a contest, as just two candidates stood for the two seats. Wilberforce had won his previous four elections this way.

Wilberforce was therefore surprised and somewhat disturbed to discover that a third candidate, Walter Fawkes, was standing this time. Actually having to fight an election would mean spending money and, like Clarkson, Wilberforce was not a very wealthy man. Some of his opponents were counting on him withdrawing due to lack of funds, but fortunately his situation was helped when Prime Minister Grenville made it known that he preferred Wilberforce and Fawkes to Lascelles. Although abolition was an issue in the election, Wilberforce's friendship with Lascelles meant that it was Fawkes who attacked the latter's ownership of slaves on his plantations in the West Indies. Both Wilberforce and Fawkes were supported by Clarkson and other Committee members who wrote to people in Yorkshire urging them to vote for those in favour of abolition. In the end, Lascelles withdrew from the election, leaving Wilberforce to be elected 'by acclaim' alongside Fawkes.

Results elsewhere increased the number of Grenville's supporters in the Commons and with this success behind him, the Prime Minister moved to end the slave trade. Aware that most opposition had previously come from the House of Lords, in January 1807 he arranged that the abolition bill start there to avoid a repetition of the situation that had occurred before: a bill arriving late in the Parliamentary year and running out of time due to delaying tactics. Grenville was also helped by a succession of people he appointed to government jobs after the election who were keen to show how loyal they were to the Prime Minister. The combined effect of these measures was that by February, the bill had been passed by the Lords by 100 votes to 34, and the debate moved to the Commons. Clarkson expressed his feelings to the cause's supporters around Britain: 'My joy is so full & my gratitude so great ... that I can only give you the plain and simple statement of our brilliant victory.

The Committee hired rooms in Downing Street, close to Parliament, and began meeting MPs to persuade them to vote for abolition. After the disappointments of the past, they were naturally a little anxious about the result, but in the early hours of the 24th February 1807, the Commons voted by 283 to just 16 to abolish the slave trade. Again, Clarkson wrote to the Committee's supporters: 'our efforts were blessed by Providence last night ... I want words to express the joy I feel ... I shall attend a Committee to day to deliberate upon a Plan for securing our Victory after which I shall leave London, with a Heart full of gratitude to the Parent of all Mercies that he had been pleased thus to render a Portion of my Life useful to my oppressed fellow creatures'.

After another, final, vote in the House of Lords in March, Prime Minister Grenville declared abolition to be the 'most glorious measure, that had ever been adopted by any legislative body in the world'. Once both Houses of Parliament have agreed on a bill, the last step before it becomes an Act of Parliament (a law) is for the sovereign to give it their Royal assent. Today, this is a formality, but at the time the King could, and sometimes would, refuse to agree. George III had recently demanded that Grenville resign as Prime Minister over the lifting of certain laws discriminating against Roman Catholics, and Clarkson was worried that the King might reject Grenville's abolition bill. Instead, George III waited half an hour after receiving Grenville's resignation before signing the bill both Clarkson and Wilberforce had worked so hard to achieve.

The Abolition of the Slave Trade Act became law at noon on March 25th 1807, two months before the Committee's twentieth anniversary. Clarkson called the Act, 'a Magna Carta for Africa', and wrote poetically of the significance of it being signed at noon: 'Just when the sun was in its meridian [highest point] splendour to witness this august Act ... to sanction it by its most vivid and glorious beams, it was completed'. Wordsworth was also moved to write, this time a sonnet in honour of his friend, *To Thomas Clarkson*:

> Clarkson! it was an obstinate hill to climb;
> How toilsome – nay, how dire – it was by thee
> Is known; by none, perhaps so fleetingly:
> But thou, who, starting in thy fervent prime,
> Didst first lead forth that enterprise sublime,
> Hast heard the constant Voice its charge repeat,
> Which, out of thy young heart's oracular seat,
> First roused thee – O true yoke-fellow of Time,
> Duty's intrepid liegeman, see, the palm
> Is won, and by all Nations shall be worn!
> The blood-stained Writing is forever torn:
> And thou henceforth wilt have a good man's calm,
> A great man's happiness; thy zeal shall find
> Repose at length, firm friend of human kind!

The new Prime Minister, the Duke of Portland, failed to win sufficient support in Parliament, so another general election was called. Once more, Wilberforce faced two other candidates as Lascelles attempted to regain his seat, only to be opposed by Lord Milton, another abolitionist. It became 'the most uproarious, expensive election ever held in Britain'. Today, candidates are limited by law to spending no more than around seven or eight thousand pounds in an election.

In contrast, Lascelles and Milton both spent over a hundred thousand pounds each, the equivalent of more than ten million pounds today.

Again, Clarkson attempted to help his friend, writing to contacts around the country, enquiring if anyone was eligible to vote for Wilberforce in Yorkshire. 'It is absolutely necessary that he should be in Parliament,' he urged, 'in Case any Attempt should be made to reverse' the recent Act. An appeal for funds to help Wilberforce fight the election was also launched, raising over sixty thousand pounds. In the end Wilberforce managed to top the poll, spending only half the amount of his rivals. Even so, he declared that the election had left him: 'thin and old'. (Lascelles was probably feeling even worse, as he had lost the election despite spending so much money.) When the next election came, a supporter of abolition ensured that Wilberforce was elected without a contest in a pocket borough.

In His Own Words

Clarkson spent most of 1807 writing his account of the abolition campaign. While in London, he stayed in the house of William Allen, a Quaker member of the Society's committee since 1805. A young girl also living there at the time recalled many years later how she had watched Clarkson working on his book. Although he was very short-sighted, 'he never used spectacles, and when he read or wrote his nose almost touched the paper'.

The results of his endeavour were published as the *History of the Rise, Progress, and Accomplishment of the Abolition of the African Slave-Trade by the British Parliament*. Wondering if anyone would be interested, Clarkson encouraged people to buy copies before its official publication date and was very pleased when almost four thousand copies were sold in this way. He showed copies to his friends, who appreciated both its style and content. Dorothy Wordsworth 'couldn't put it down' and compared it to a great novel. Samuel Coleridge complained mildly that the first three pages were dull, but said the rest was 'deeply interesting', and compared the defeat of the slave trade to the conquests of Napoleon and Alexander the Great. Clarkson, he said, was: 'a benefactor of mankind' who 'listened exclusively to his conscience, and obeyed its voice'.

Clarkson's history of the movement concentrated on those areas he knew most about. There were long sections on his researches and travels around Britain for the Committee, and rather less on the internal workings of Parliament. The period between his 'retirement' to Ullswater and the final votes in 1807 was hardly covered at all. This focus led some people who had only just become involved in the campaign to comment that the book was partial and sought to over-emphasise Clarkson's role in the campaign. One of Wilberforce's advisers felt particularly snubbed and complained he had not received proper acknowledgement for his efforts. Wilberforce's somewhat diplomatic response was to say that in the book: 'nothing is said ... which is not true & still more is not intended to be so, yet by no means [does it cover] all that deserves commemoration'.

The book ended with Clarkson's hopes for the future, particularly the achievement of freedom for those still in slavery: 'Who knows but that emancipation, like a beautiful plant, may, in its due season, rise out of the ashes of the abolition of the Slave-trade'.

International Action

Despite the successful passage of the Abolition of the Slave Trade Act, the trade and transport of slaves continued, often with ships which flew another country's flag despite being managed from Britain. After one visit to Liverpool, Clarkson noted that such illegal activity was 'deplorably numerous'. He was determined to ensure that such behaviour was stamped out and professed: 'We now know all the tricks & subterfuges and we know the authors, we know under what flags the mischief is continued; we know the haunts of the marauders, their employers &c &c & we hope to do them away one after the other, till we have cleared the Coast.'

International action was needed and one opportunity arose with the Allies' victory over France in 1814. The Treaty of Paris which ended the war gave back some of the colonies which France had lost, but it did not insist that slavery be abolished there. Rather, it allowed France to continue trading slaves for five years. When the British Foreign Secretary reported back to the House of Commons on the treaty he had helped to draw up, Wilberforce spoke of it as 'a death warrant for thousands'.

A conference of great importance, the Congress of Vienna, was organised in November for the rulers of Europe to establish their common future. Clarkson set about persuading the individual heads of state to support the abolitionists in order to ensure that the Congress decided against slavery. While the Emperor of Russia and King of Prussia were visiting London they were presented with copies of Clarkson's evidence against the trade. When the Emperor left Britain he sailed to Calais and was visibly ill on the voyage. Dismissing the rough seas, he pointed to a picture of a slave ship in Clarkson's book saying: 'it is that book ... which has made me more sick than the sea'.

Clarkson also took part in a rally which launched a petition to Parliament. In four days, it collected 39,143 signatures. More petitions were launched around the country, with Clarkson sending two thousand letters around the network established by the Committee. His strong campaigning spirit was still thriving and he wrote to Catherine: 'My dearest Love in a week we shall have 5 or 600 [petitions], and in a subsequent 7 days, 3 times as many more. If we exert our Voices, we are sure to find a Change at the ensuing Congress. If we do not we must leave Matters as they are, i.e. Desolation & Misery to Africa for 5 years'. In total, over three-quarters of a million signatures were gathered. The Prince Regent wrote to the new King of France to say that he would regard it as a personal favour if the French abolished the slave trade too.

Clarkson was determined to go to Vienna for the Congress, but Wilberforce persuaded him against it, saying that the result should be regarded as the success or failure of the British government, not Clarkson. As an alternative, Clarkson insisted on going to Paris, to build support against the slave trade there. Most of the leading members of La Societé des Amis des Noirs had died, either during the bloody phases of the French Revolution or during the long war with the rest of Europe. One royalist member he met in France had himself just returned from a long exile in Britain. He complained that Clarkson was meeting with the Marquis de Lafayette, who had fought with the Americans in their War of Independence against the British and then served both sides during the French Revolution and subsequent war. Clarkson's reply was characteristic of his single-mindedness: 'I know but two classes of persons – the friends and enemies of Africa. All the friends of Africa are my friends, whatever they may be besides. You and Monsieur Lafayette are the same in my eyes'. Indeed, Lafayette, an old friend, had bought a plantation in Guiana in 1786 and freed its slaves over several years.

Clarkson also met Britain's ambassador to Paris, the Duke of Wellington, who pointed out that Britain's demand to end the slave trade was seen as serving her own purposes. Since many in France still hated Britain, Clarkson need to concentrate on ensuring that the horrors of slave trade were even more despised. Wellington had been told by the King of France himself that he could: 'no more abolish the trade against the will of the people of France than the King of England can continue it against the will of the people of England'.

Moved to more direct action, Clarkson searched the bookshops of Paris for a copy of the original translation of his books which *La Societé* had published twenty-five years earlier. The French censor gave permission for a new edition in record time and Wellington used his diplomatic privileges to have the printing plates of *The Print*, so famous in Britain, brought to France so that it too could be published. Copies of both were soon sent to every important figure in Paris. Acknowledging the co-operation of the British government in helping his efforts, Clarkson firmly believed that the petitions had been decisive in gaining influence: 'No other satisfactory answer can be given why [they were] so apparently indifferent to the subject when the treaty [of Paris] was made and why so interested since'.

In further talks with Wellington, Clarkson discovered that Britain was prepared to pay Portugal and Spain to stop their trade in slaves. Since France was not prepared to stop its trade unconditionally, Clarkson suggested an extra concession such as returning another one of the islands taken from them during the war. In the end, no such deal was struck. More disappointment followed when in Vienna, the Congress declined to commit itself to action to end the slave trade, although it accepted that this practice was: 'the desolation of Africa, the degradation of Europe, and the afflicting scourge of humanity'.

In 1815, Napoleon returned from exile in Elba for his second, short, reign in France. One of his first acts was to say he would abolish the slave trade, though he had failed to do so before 1814. However, no action was taken toward this goal and following Napoleon's final defeat at Waterloo, Clarkson waited for the new French government to either confirm or withdraw the abolition proposal. In fact, they chose to do neither, effectively leaving the trade in place.

A second great gathering of heads of state was scheduled for September 1815 in Paris. Although Clarkson was in the process of moving house, he travelled once more to Paris with the specific intention of meeting with the Russian Emperor. He was granted a private audience with the Emperor who told Clarkson that he was honoured that he had come from Britain especially to meet with him. Reading Clarkson's books had increased his personal determination to: 'wipe away such a pestilence from the face of the Earth'. The Emperor had argued for action against the slave trade at Vienna, but had been unable to convince all nations to agree. After their discussion, the two men then made their own agreement that Clarkson would write with his suggestions on future work.

Insurrection on a slave ship. W. Fox, *Brief history,* 1851.

Cutting sugar cane in Antigua 1823

Pitt addresses the House of Commons. Wilberforce sits in front of the right-hand pillar.
Painting by K A Hickel

Against Slavery Itself

In 1822, the next stage of the British abolition campaign was launched; this time it was directed against the whole institution of slavery rather than simply the trade in human lives. A new organisation was founded, the Society for Mitigating and Gradually Abolishing the State of Slavery throughout the British Dominions. Although he had played no part in its foundation, Clarkson was nominated onto its committee, being told 'we have ... put thy name on the Committee in the midst of those, with whom thou has always delighted to work'. The new committee asked Clarkson to help organise their campaign, 'We need him much,' they wrote to Catherine, explaining that everyone else was engrossed in other matters. Clarkson tested public opinion on the opposition to slavery with a petition in Suffolk and found people were very willing to sign. 'I have no where been refused,' he wrote, 'It seems only to ask & to have'.

Clarkson was already working on a pamphlet regarding this subject, its content summed up by its title: *Thoughts on the Necessity for Improving the Condition of Slaves in the British Colonies, with a View to their Ultimate Emancipation, and the Practicality, Safety, and Advantages of the Latter Measure.* Perhaps mindful of the example of Haiti, he wrote that a gradual progress towards freedom was necessary. He wrote that nothing would be 'so insane' as to go directly to emancipation without a process of education and preparation.

Although it had been over a decade since the end of the legal slave trade, slavery remained in the nation's mind. The continuing attention was largely due to the slaves themselves, many of whom, despite being semi-skilled, had found themselves labouring back in the sugar cane fields formerly reserved for women and the new slaves from Africa. Despite the increasingly harsh repressive measures enforced by the plantation owners, the slaves' resentment erupted into revolts. The public were outraged as rebellious slaves were massacred on island after island and they heard how for each white person killed, hundreds of slaves were murdered. The violence and brutality of the slave owners ensured that the people of Britain were increasingly sick of slavery.

By June 1823, a plan had been drawn up to re-establish the Committee's network of local working parties, with Clarkson once more touring Britain to advise on their establishment. Back on the road campaigning for the cause of abolition, friends noted that he looked ten years younger. By the following summer, eight hundred towns were covered by local groups and 777 petitions had been sent to Parliament. Clarkson was confident that: 'It is everyone's opinion, that SLAVERY is to fall, this idea pervades all England & Wales'.

Despite this level of public support, the government refused to adopt the policy of emancipation, preferring 'amelioration', which merely meant making the lives of slaves better. Furthermore, they failed to pass laws in Britain to ensure that serious improvements were made, choosing to wait for the colonies in the West Indies to act. Some progress was made, but neither side was left content: slave owners complained that the reforms cost money and abolitionists wanted progress towards full emancipation. Throughout this period, Clarkson continued to make great efforts to build support, even though his only formal position was as chair of the local Ipswich committee. 'If I work hard today,' he told a friend, 'I shall finish my three hundred and twelve letters which I am writing ... about petitions'. For the first time, he also encouraged women to sign petitions.

In 1830, the 'gradualist' approach to emancipation was abandoned by the new Anti-Slavery Society. At a large meeting in London, Wilberforce and Clarkson paid each other tribute. Clarkson moved that Wilberforce chair the meeting, 'as the great leader in our cause'. Wilberforce, in his last public appearance, replied that there was: 'no person more dear to me than my valued friend and fellow-labourer'. Looking back to the start of his work against slavery, he recalled when: 'we made the first step towards that great object, the completion of which is the purpose of our assembling this day'. The movement continued to grow until there were more than thirteen hundred local abolition committees. When asked to distribute petitions calling for the 'entire Abolition of Colonial Slavery', an astonishing 5484 were sent to Parliament. Although women could not vote they did sign petitions and, in 1833, over 187,000 women indicated their disapproval of slavery in a 'great feather-bed of a petition' that took four sturdy MPs to haul into parliament. Over 300,000 people gave up sugar thereby reducing the slavers' income by £20,000 in three months. The campaign against slavery united Britain more than any other issue.

When the motion was finally debated in the House of Commons, the argument became not whether emancipation would happen, but under what terms. In 1833, Parliament decided that slavery would end on 1st August 1834. All children under six would be freed at once, while other slaves would become 'apprentices', working for their former masters without pay for some years before winning full freedom, although Antigua and Bermuda decided to free all their slaves immediately. In return for emancipation, slave owners were to be given twenty million pounds in compensation. While some people were dissatisfied with these conditions, and asked why the real victims, the slaves, were not given the money, Clarkson was 'inexpressibly delighted' at the result of his campaigning and concluded that: 'The twenty millions will have been well laid out, if it will secure the cordial cooperation of the planters'.

Ironically, the King who signed the new Act was William IV, the former Duke of Clarence, who had earlier attacked abolitionists as being 'either fanatics or hypocrites.' However, even the King's approval did not move all other countries to follow. France finally banned its slave trade in 1848. In the United States, it would take the long and bloody American Civil War (1861-1865) before the four million slaves were freed.

By the end of the Atlantic trade in slaves, eleven million Africans had been brought to the Americas as slaves. Since so many died on board ship or whilst being herded to the African coast, it is estimated that the trade had enslaved up to twenty-four million men, women and children. Even after 1834, some of these continued to suffer as slaves. Around a hundred Jamaicans, who had been imprisoned for offences such as running away from their plantations, were transported to Australia, via Britain. Twenty-four of them had been born in Africa, survived one crossing of the Atlantic Ocean, slavery in Jamaica, and another crossing of the Atlantic to a prison ship in Britain before making their final 12,000 mile voyage to the convict colonies near Sydney.

Although the law of 1833 was crucial in changing the lives of millions of Africans, the debates, delays and compromises which characterised the British Parliament's slow journey towards full abolition and emancipation must always be considered alongside the protests and actions of the enslaved Africans themselves. We should not be taken in by a whitewashed view of history which tells us that the abolitionists alone put an end to slavery, as it was the Africans who also brought about their own freedom and the collapse of the slave system, too often at the cost of their own lives.

The Deaths of the
Two Great Campaigners

By the time that his life's ambition had been realised, Clarkson was an old man and almost blinded by cataracts in his eyes. For a man who had published such fine material throughout his life, it was a particular sadness that he was unable: 'to read a word of what I have written'. The news of Wilberforce's death in July 1833 had to be broken to him gently, but on hearing it Clarkson locked himself in his study and was heard 'in an agony of grief weeping and uttering loud lamentations'. 'We have long acted together in the greatest cause which ever engaged the efforts of public men,' Wilberforce had written to Clarkson and he had also acknowledged at the meeting in 1830 that Clarkson had been working on abolition long before he had taken it up in Parliament.

Given the alliance and admiration which existed between these two men, it was especially unjust that Wilberforce's sons went out of their way to ignore or belittle Clarkson's achievements in their biography of their father. The sons were encouraged by James Stephen, the son of the adviser to Wilberforce who had thought that his work had not been acknowledged in Clarkson's own history of the campaign against the slave trade. Stephen declared: 'I believe Clarkson did as much to frustrate and delay the abolition, as he ever did to promote it,' and advised them that it was an 'urgent public duty' to put down the man who had tried to claim all the credit for himself.

The brothers should have realised that this was untrue when they read Clarkson's reply to their request for help: 'I am glad that you are going to write your Father's Life,' he wrote, adding, 'but it will be a most laborious Task ... for his private life was as full of glorious Labour and as splendid as his public one'. These were hardly the words of someone who sought to claim sole credit for abolition.

When the biography, *Life of William Wilberforce*, was published in 1838 it caused outrage in many quarters. The *Sunday Times* responded with the comment that: 'Everyone of common sense knows that the merit was Clarkson's and not Wilberforce's'. Even the *Christian Observer*, the newspaper of the same evangelical faith as Wilberforce, could not agree with the way the book ignored Clarkson in favour of Wilberforce and stated that: 'Both were earliest, and both were best, in their respective spheres'.

Clarkson, also received recognition from other quarters and was conspicuously granted the Freedom of the City of London for: 'the merit of originating ... the triumph of the great struggle for the deliverance of the enslaved African'. Two years later, at the first joint meeting of the world's anti-slavery movements, he was voted president of the convention and acknowledged as the 'originator' of Britain's Committee for Effecting the Abolition of the Slave Trade.

Two of the Irish delegation to the convention wrote to a friend about the reception given to Clarkson in a way which leaves no doubt as to the respect in which he was held by all there. "We this day saw the man best worth seeing in England – Thomas Clarkson," wrote one. "He came into the meeting at about half-past ten, leaning on [two other campaigners] and followed by his daughter-in-law and grandson. ... T.C. spoke, and a more interesting scene could not be; – and literally there was hardly a dry eye in the house whilst Clarkson was speaking."

Another noted the reaction from a freed slave, "Afterwards an emancipated West Indian came and shook hands with [Clarkson] and spoke well. 'Look at me and go on,' he said again and again."

Stephen was reported to be: 'staggered ... by the apparent unanimity with which parts of the Book ... would appear to be condemned,' and advised Wilberforce's sons to revise it for the second edition. They agreed, but still omitted Clarkson from the list of members of his Committee. It was not until 1844 that Clarkson receive a private apology from Wilberforce's sons, one then an Archbishop, the other a Bishop. They wrote to him saying: 'we think ourselves bound to acknowledge that we were wrong in the manner in which we treated you in the Memoir of our Father', but did not revise the book further.

Clarkson's work for the cause was not over. The campaign against slavery in the United States was just beginning and its leaders looked to Clarkson for advice and support. The cause was divided into factions, a damaging state of affairs that Clarkson had always avoided in Britain. One faction, the American Colonization Society, wanted to transport the slaves, including those born in America, to the African state of Liberia. Its leader published highly selective extracts from a letter from Clarkson to make it appear that he supported this plan, editing out the sections calling for freed American slaves to be given citizenship of the United States. In response, the leader of the other faction, William Lloyd Garrison, sailed across the Atlantic in 1833 to meet Clarkson. Garrison was the energetic and controversial founder of the *Liberator* newspaper and the New England Anti-Slave Society. His first editorial in the *Liberator* echoed the attitude of Charles James Fox many years earlier: 'On this subject I do not wish to think, to speak or write with moderation. No! no! Tell a man whose house is on fire, to give a moderate alarm; tell him to moderately rescue his wife from the hands of the ravisher; tell the mother to gradually extricate her babe from the fire into which it has fallen – but urge me not to use moderation in a cause like the present'.

Clarkson would not take sides in the dispute. Unless it could be proved that the American Colonization Society would not further the cause of abolition, he would not condemn them. For once, Garrison was 'awed into silence' and he returned to America without the endorsement he desired. It took some years before Clarkson was convinced that the American Colonization Society was indeed an obstacle to abolition.

In the meantime, Garrison's tactics and fundamentalism had split the American campaign again. He suggested that the states which banned slavery leave the United States, even though this was fraught with danger. (In the end, it was the states which wished to keep slavery who attempted to leave the union some years later and the result was the American Civil War, 1861-1865.) Garrison also widened his political objectives to include opposition to war and to the death penalty, as well as to involve women directly in the campaign. Even though Clarkson personally approved of all these new measures, he despaired of the damage they caused his primary concern, the abolition of slavery: 'This cause is a pure and holy cause, and must be kept unspotted as far as possible ... from all political as well as fanatical excitements'.

Although no-one but himself would have objected if he had retired from the cause, Clarkson continued to write letters and pamphlets on a wide range of points, from condemning the American Clergy who supported slavery to opposing the admission of the State of Texas to the United States unless it first banned slavery. 'Would you believe it possible ... that now on the eve of going into the eighty-fourth year of my age, I should have been obliged to work eight hours a day for the last three years,' Clarkson asked in a letter to a friend in 1843. In 1845, he returned to one of his earliest concerns, the predicaments faced by British sailors for his final publication, *Grievances of our Mercantile Seamen, a National and Crying Evil*.

Catherine and Thomas Clarkson celebrated their fiftieth wedding anniversary together in January 1846. He died peacefully on 26th September that year, surrounded by a number of his friends. In contrast to Wilberforce, Sharp and other leaders of the abolition movement who are buried in Westminster Abbey alongside Britain's other great public figures, Clarkson had insisted on a plain, Quaker-style, funeral. He is buried in the churchyard at Playford, near Ipswich, where he had his last home.

Clarkson had guided the British campaign against slavery from its very beginnings to its end, and his work had influenced abolition movements around the world. In 1996, 150 years after his death, a plaque will finally be unveiled in Westminster Abbey to remember and celebrate the extraordinary life of Thomas Clarkson, 'one of the noblest of Englishmen'.

Etching of Playford Hall, near Ipswich, with Thomas Clarkson, autographed by himself less than a month before he died in 1846 (aged 87). He had lived here for the last 30 years of his life and he was buried in the family vault at Playford churchyard, a simple resting place for a man who called himself 'half a Quaker'

Cotton growing was immensely profitable in America, planters' demands for more slaves prolonged the illegal slave-trade until the South was defeated in the Civil War in 1865

DESIGN FOR THE CLARKSON MEMORIAL.
WISBECH.

The Clarkson Memorial, Wisbech. Designed by Sir Gilbert Scott RA, the monument was funded by public subscription and unveiled in 1881 by the Rt Hon Bouverie Brand MP, Speaker of the House of Commons. This is a perspective drawing from the original design: it was later modified by increasing the height of the upper gothic gallery to make the statue taller by about six feet

Slavery Today

There can be no doubt that the institution of slavery, which was formally abolished in Britain's empire over 150 years ago, has shaped the consciousness, the cultural mixture and the economic situation of the contemporary world. Our ways of relating to and representing peoples of other cultures are still guided by many of the pernicious stereotypes employed to justify slavery. Racial discrimination and the suffering this causes are still major issues which the Western world must face. The diversity of ethnic and cultural groups in the contemporary societies of Europe and the US is largely the result of the African diaspora (scattering of peoples) which slavery and colonisation enforced. Slavery was a major aspect of the economic and social development of many, if not most, countries and the divides between rich and poor today often echo those established in the eighteenth and nineteenth centuries.

However, slavery not only continues to affect the contemporary world in these ways. Ships no longer cross the Atlantic packed with slaves from Africa but, unfortunately, this does not mean that slavery has ended. Indeed, there are probably more slaves alive today than at any other time in history. Anti-Slavery International, the descendant of Clarkson's campaigners and the world's oldest human rights organisation, estimates that two hundred million people are living as slaves today – three and half times the population of the United Kingdom.

The United Nations' Slavery Convention, which was first adopted by the League of Nations in 1926, defines slavery as the status or condition of a person over whom any or all of the powers attaching to the right of ownership are exercised. This means that people are considered to be slaves if they can be sold by one employer to another, or are forced to do something against their will, or cannot change jobs even when they want to. Slaves can be, and are, men and women, girls and boys.

Today, some slaves are made to work without pay by their governments in 'forced labour', while others are like the slaves of Clarkson's day, completely owned by someone who treats them as a 'chattel' or possession. In some parts of the world, women in 'servile marriages' are the property of their husbands and are counted among their possessions, with no individual status or freedom. In many places, 'child labour' is common and children are made to work for nothing or very little, rather than being free to go to school or play with their friends.

Bonded labour, which has existed for thousands of years and was used to build the pyramids of ancient Egypt, remains one of the most common forms of slavery today. This system of slavery operates on the practice of selling yourself, or members of your family, into bonded labour to pay off a debt. Most people need to borrow money at some point in their lives. Some people borrow to buy their home, while others borrow to buy expensive luxury goods. Many poor people have to borrow simply to buy basic items like food and clothing. As these people are poor, the banks do not believe they will be able to repay the debt. It is a cruel reality that the very poorest people often have the hardest time trying to borrow money and are often forced to rely on unscrupulous money-lenders, who charge very high rates of interest. With these loans, the amount owed can soon be many times the original amount borrowed and this means that the borrower has to sell themselves for many years, often their whole lifetime.

Even death offers no escape, because the debt continues. It is estimated that many bonded labourers in India are enslaved by loans inherited from their parents, while others were sold as children when their parents could not afford to feed them. Some children are simply kidnapped and sold to unscrupulous businesses.

It is estimated that there are around fifty million child labourers in India, Pakistan and Bangladesh. All around the world, child workers are popular with unprincipled employers because they are easier to control than adults and are unable to demand proper wages or working conditions. Child bonded labourers, who are often given nothing but their food and somewhere to sleep for their tireless work, are particularly attractive to such immoral employers. Denied the basic human rights of an education, time to play and loving attention, these children live miserable lives on farms and in factories and brothels.

Many such children work in the brick industry, forming the bricks from mud, carrying them and turning them in the sun as they bake. Despite the heavy nature of this work, they are paid a tiny amount per brick produced. Illness is common because of their unhealthy working conditions, yet any time off means the debt rises because they are still charged for their food and accommodation. Still more child bonded labourers work on farms. The younger children look after animals or pick weeds, while older children do the hard physical work. Their lives are not so far removed from those of the young slaves working on the plantations in the West Indies two centuries ago. Again, the lack of consideration for safety means that many children are injured in accidents, and if they are unable to work as a result of injury they face a very uncertain future. Others work long hours in the carpet industry; in cramped, dusty rooms, their health inevitably suffers. It is sometimes said that children make the best carpets because of their small fingers, but in reality trained adults produce the finest work. The carpets made by child bonded labour are not produced to fulfil the demand for quality, but to satisfy the West's demand for cheap handmade goods.

Just as many people listened to Clarkson when he asked them to boycott slave-produced sugar, it is important that people today refuse to buy products made by child slaves, many of which are on sale in Britain's shops. A few years ago, publicity about the treatment of animals in testing goods like cosmetics shocked many people and there was public demand for cosmetics that had not been tested in this way. Companies now compete to offer such 'cruelty-free' products; their profits remain steady and the animals do not suffer. In the same way, each individual can help end slavery by finding out how the things they use and the foods they eat are made. If you discover goods which are made by slaves, refuse to buy them and tell others why. The actions of each one of us feed into larger patterns of behaviour and structures of production and consumption. By changing our own buying habits we can affect much wider change and make a lasting difference to others.

One particular scheme called Rugmark has been organised by groups fighting slavery in the Indian subcontinent. Carpets which are made without child labour are awarded a special mark. If buyers choose wisely, then carpets with the Rugmark will sell better than those without and this will encourage other carpet factory owners to stop using child labour, so that they too can qualify for the Rugmark. The factories which are awarded the Rugmark are regularly inspected to make sure that they comply with the rules concerning working conditions and child labour.

In order to demonstrate our conviction to see the end of slavery and to improve the conditions of these people's lives, we need to accept that we have to pay a fair price for the goods bought from poor countries. Insisting on an unrealistically low price for a handmade carpet, for example, brings a hidden cost in the suffering of children who work and live in appalling conditions in order to satisfy the greed of their owners and the consumers in richer countries.

While such commercial schemes are vital to the abolition of child slavery, the deep causes of this problem also need to be addressed. When adult workers are paid properly, their children have no need to work and support the family, and thus they can go to school. Without the severe poverty which afflicts whole areas of the world today, families would not be tempted to take out the dangerous loans which lead to bonded labour, or to sell their children into this system of slavery. It would also be harder for factory owners to bribe police into ignoring the anti-slavery laws.

It is clear that the fight against slavery is linked with the need to provide education for all. In some countries there is a high level of illiteracy and this means that many bonded labour contracts are never written down. As a consequence, it is almost impossible to prove the terms of the debt or its repayment, and the contracts can easily be altered in favour of the factory owners. The campaign to provide universal education is a long-term goal which all who seek to abolish slavery and exploitation today must support.

The life of Thomas Clarkson shows us that one dedicated person can make a real difference to the lives of millions. If you would like to join the continuing campaign against slavery today, please write to:

Anti-Slavery International
The Stableyard, Broomgrove Road, London SW9 9TL
Tel: 0171-924 9555 Fax: 0171-738 4110

In the USA:
American Anti-Slavery Group
PO Box 441612, W Somerville, MA 02144
Tel: (617) 278 4324

In Australia:
Anti-Slavery Society Australia
GPO Box 438C, Victoria 3001
Tel: (03) 608 8342 Fax: (03) 601 6437

Further Reading on Slave Narratives
and the Black Population in Britain

Paul Edwards, ed., Equiano's Travels (London: Heinemann, 1967)

Paul Edwards & David Dabydeen, eds., Black Writers in Britain 1760-1890 (Edinburgh, Edinburgh University Press, 1991)

Paul Edwards & James Walvin, Black Personalities in the Era of the Slave Trade (London: Macmillan, 1983)

Shyllon, Black People in Britain 1555-1833 (Oxford: Oxford University Press, 1977)

Peter Fryer, Staying Power (London: Pluto Press, 1984)

Moira Ferguson, ed., The History of Mary Prince, A West Indian Slave, Related by Herself (London: Pandora, 1987, first published 1831)

Henry Louis Gates, Jr., ed., Narrative of the Life of Frederick Douglass, an American Slave (New York: Mentor, 1987, first published 1845)

Harriet Jacobs, Incidents in the Life of a Slave Girl (Oxford: Oxford University Press, 1988, first published 1861)

A photograph from Brazil shows children working to produce charcoal in Maranhao. They are members of families forced to work in terrible conditions and are kept there through debts incurred to kiln owners

This girl is a member of a family of debt-bonded labourers working at a Pakistani kiln, having been forced to repay a debt to the kiln owner - probably money borrowed to pay for medical treatment, a marriage or a death. Only the owner of the kiln has control over the amount of work necessary to repay the debt

Thomas Clarkson addresses the Anti-Slavery Convention held in London during June 1840

Medallion commemorating the convention